THE
WOLF ECONOMY
AWAKENS

Praise for *The Wolf Economy Awakens*

"Nylander's book is a must read for Asia enthusiasts, as he once again gets under the skin of an economy and reveals the fascinating complexities and personalities that make it tick.

As one of the last genuine wild outposts in the modern world, and straddling the politics of both China and Russia, Mongolia is an economy that is barely understood, seriously under-reported and sitting on a literal goldmine."

—*Rob Carnell, head of research and chief economist, Asia-Pacific, ING Bank (Singapore)*

"I have read all about Mongolia, and have lived and run a business in the country for three decades. Johan Nylander's book is by far my favourite read on contemporary Mongolia, and offers the best summary of Mongolia's post-pandemic challenges.

The book is balanced and well narrated, and contains many conversations with prominent Mongolians of all persuasions and from all walks of life. It's revealing for me even as a long-term resident."

—*Jan Wigsten, CEO, 360° Mongolia (Ulaanbaatar)*

"Johan Nylander, a journalist with deep Asia experience, has interviewed Mongolian nomads, tech entrepreneurs, the country's Prime Minister and opposition leaders. He's well suited to write this book which asks this question: will Mongolia escape endemic corruption and the resource trap and become Asia's next boom economy while maintaining its admirable democracy?

Well worth the read as Nylander ably integrates analysis and on-the-ground reporting talking to some of the fascinating

Mongolians caught up in this epic story, the outcome of which matters for the region and the world."

—*Dexter Roberts, senior fellow,*
The Atlantic Council's Asia Security Initiative (Washington DC)

"I never thought I would be caught up by a book on Mongolia, where I have never been, as if I were reading a detective story, but that is exactly what Johan Nylander has achieved with his amazing book, namely to incite my interest in the country, which happens to be a vibrant democracy landlocked between Russia and China. This 'wolf economy,' thanks to its vast natural resources, is transforming itself into a start-up nation and proof of what you can become if you really want it, no matter the geography."

— *Alicia García Herrero, chief economist,*
Asia Pacific, Natixis (Hong Kong)

"Johan is one of the best storytellers and writers I know."

—*Akash Karia, global keynote speaker*
and bestselling author (Hong Kong)

THE
WOLF ECONOMY
AWAKENS

MONGOLIA'S FIGHT FOR DEMOCRACY, AND A GREEN AND DIGITAL FUTURE

JOHAN NYLANDER

HKU
PRESS
香港大學出版社

Hong Kong University Press
The University of Hong Kong
Pok Fu Lam Road
Hong Kong
https://hkupress.hku.hk

© 2024 Hong Kong University Press

ISBN 978-988-8842-84-1 (*Paperback*)

British Library Cataloguing-in-Publication Data
A catalogue record for this book is available from the British Library.

Editing: Kenny Hodgart
Cover design: Darren Hayward
Layout and formatting: Pankaj Runthala
Cover photos: Johan Nylander/ Gobi Cashmere

Digitally printed

For more information and gallery
wolfeconomy.asia

Contents

Introduction 1

About the author 11

1. Visionaries and peacemakers 13

2. Climbing mining's value chain 81

3. Silicon steppe: A green tech giant stirs 117

4. Empowering the great outdoors 163

Introduction

Growing up in the town of Berkh in eastern Mongolia in the 1980s could be rough. The fluorspar mine was the heart of the community, and Mongolian miners worked side by side with Russians and Kazaks. Prisoners sentenced to hard labor were also sent down the shafts.

Located around 500 kilometers east of the capital, Ulaanbaatar, some 10,000 people called Berkh home in those days—a lot for a Mongolian administrative district, or *sum*. The facades of the workers' living quarters were decorated with the hammer and sickle, the Soviet symbol. There were a few restaurants, all serving traditional meaty dishes and vodka, and during the weekends the local cultural center opened its doors for music and dancing. In winter, temperatures would reach as low as minus 40 degrees Celsius, and the sky would turn dark from the burning of coal for heat. Outside the village, the dry grassy steppe stretched endlessly in all directions, occupied by roaming horses, cows and goats. The huff and puff of the mine, located just a few hundred meters from the town center, was like endless background music.

On warm summer days, living close to the countryside could be idyllic. But the harsh mining environment—a macho habitat that bore the rigors of heavy drinking—was not always easy. In fact, the threat of violence was never far away.

Late one afternoon, an 11-year-old boy was attacked by a drunken miner. The boy tried to fight the man off as best as he could, but the miner was strong and kept coming at him. "I'm going to kill you," he shouted. He even tried to smash a bottle over the child's head. The situation looked bad—very bad. Then, out of nowhere, one of the boy's best friends came running, and together they fended the drunken man off and escaped to safety.

The following day, the two boys—Anar and Oyuka—were sitting on a stone wall in the morning sunshine when the miner walked past them. He looked embarrassed and humiliated. "Come here, and we'll beat you again," they shouted at him with newfound confidence. The miner lowered his gaze, apologized quietly, and walked off. The children had won the battle.

Soon after the incident, the boy who had been attacked, Anar, moved to another town with his family, and the two friends lost contact. It would take another 30 years until they reconnected, at a meeting in Ulaanbaatar. By then, the fluorspar mine had closed, the population of Berkh had fallen to a fraction of its level during the boom years, and most of the restaurants, shops, and local businesses had shut down. The hammer and sickle on the facades of the old working quarters now seemed emblematic of the collapse of the Communist regime, and Mongolia had become a liberated democracy.

The two boys, meanwhile, had grown into men: both had just turned 40 and had families of their own. And what brought them together at this meeting in the capital was that they had both, in different ways, become vital drivers and even symbols of a new Mongolia.

Anar Chinbaatar is today the country's most famous tech startup entrepreneur. His cutting-edge fintech group AND Global has branches and investors across Asia, as well as in the San Francisco Bay Area, and he's aiming for "unicorn" status (a valuation of $1 billion or more.) He's also one of the "sharks" in the local version of the American business reality television series *Shark Tank*, a celebrated motivational speaker and TED Talker, and a major sponsor of several NGOs aimed at nurturing the next generation of young tech wizards.

Luvsannamsrai "Oyuka" Oyun-Erdene, meanwhile, is the prime minister of Mongolia. When he was inaugurated in 2021, at the age of 40, he was one of the youngest leaders in the world. A graduate of Harvard University, where he studied public policy, he spent his early career fighting for social development and campaigning against corruption, and he is the architect of Vision 2050, a long-term roadmap for modernizing Mongolia's economy and creating a greener, more equal, more digital society.

The two men were (re)introduced by officials from the newly established Ministry of Digital Development and Communications. Unaware of the history the two men shared, the ministry wanted the prime minister to get to know one of the country's foremost tech innovators. Little did they know that they were about to spark fond reminiscences of the pair's younger days. Recalling their shared experiences in Berkh, they embraced and laughed about the drunken miner and about how "tough" they had been at the age of 11. Neither did it escape them that they had both come a long way.

This tale of Anar and Oyuka is more than just an amusing anecdote. It also tells us quite a lot about the overall development of Mongolia.

First, it's a story about social mobility. In Mongolia, you don't have to be born into a wealthy or powerful elite to get to the top. Of course, rising above the socioeconomic circumstances you're born into is never exactly easy, but not being defined by your parents' status is often an important indicator of a healthy, functional society and economy. There has traditionally been a concentration of power in Mongolia, a few dozen families said to control much of the country's politics and business. That two boys from a rough mining town were able to break through barriers and succeed—on parallel tracks—speaks well, however, of Mongolia as a place of equity and opportunity.

During a trip to Berkh in mid-September 2022, I visited the local primary school the prime minister attended as a child. With its long corridors and tiny desks, it looked like almost any other primary school in the world. And, as in other schools, photos of notable alumni were proudly displayed in a glass cabinet. Among the former students to have "made it" were not only the prime minister but an Olympic athlete and a famous wrestler.

In the classroom in which Oyun-Erdene had been schooled, I spoke to the boy who now sat at his old desk—a privilege of which the boy was unaware. "This is where the prime minister sat," I said to him. "Now it's your desk. You never know what can happen if you're ready to study and work hard." I could see his eyes open wider, as the thought occurred to him, possibly for the first time, that someday he too might lead his country.

Another thing the story of Berkh reveals, however, is about the shortcomings of mining dependency, or the so-called "resource curse." It highlights how quickly a boom town can become a run-down rust-belt area when the resources it depends on run out—something that's especially true when not enough money is reinvested back into the local community during lucrative times. This is true, of course, not just on the local level but for whole nations too.

Investments in diversified industries, such as agriculture and tourism, are finally being made in Berkh today. It should and could have happened decades ago, but as the saying goes, "The best time to plant a tree was 20 years ago; the second-best time is today." Similarly, the Mongolian government today aims to diversify the country's economy, cut mining dependency, and scale up in other sectors such as technology and green energy.

A third aspect of the story is collaboration. Only together could the boys fight off the drunk miner. During an interview I was granted with the prime minister, he referred to Badmaanyambuugiin Bat-Erdene, the greatest traditional Mongolian wrestler of the modern era. "Alone, no one could beat him; but two men—no, perhaps six men—could take him down," he said with a chuckle.

On a more serious note, he also referred to an old folk tale that all children in Mongolia are told. It's the story of Alan Gua, "Alun the Beauty," a mythical female figure who features in the nation's oldest surviving work of literature, *The Secret History of the Mongols*. It goes something like this:

Queen Alan Gua had five sons, but none of them got along with the others. The queen was at a loss as to how to resolve the siblings' conflicts. Then she called her children together and handed each of them an arrow. She instructed them to break the arrows, and they all succeeded immediately. She then gathered five arrows together in a bundle and asked them to break them, but none were able. "Sons, you are like these arrows," she said. "If you are on your own, you will break easily. But when you are together, you are unbreakable."

From this tale, one can draw many different lessons about communication, leadership, and conflict resolution—and about solidarity and unity.

According to several reports and indicators, today Mongolia stands on the edge of becoming Asia's next boom economy and of replicating the progress made in many other nations in the region.

I've been covering economic and social development in Asia (including Mongolia) for the last two decades, and in that time I've witnessed mind-blowing development occur across the continent. I've seen disruptors from Seoul to Jakarta create astonishing new economic value that has pushed the region to the forefront of global economic expansion. I've seen China transform itself from a polluted industrial complex to a tech superpower. And I've seen the countries of Southeast Asia become some of the world's most vibrant consumer markets, people using "super apps" in their daily lives that have scarcely been imagined in the West. I've also interviewed legendary founders such as Alibaba's Jack Ma, Huawei's Ren Zhengfei, and Stan Shih of Acer, as well as the leaders of many of Asia's top startups and venture capital firms—and they all agree the future belongs to Asia in economic power. The global gravity of GDP (gross domestic product; put simply, where you have most economic activity in the world) tilts no longer to the West but to the East, just as it did during the era of the Silk Road. In purchasing power, Asia is set to overtake (if it hasn't already) the rest of the world combined, marking the "inflection point when the continent becomes the new center of the world," according to the *Financial Times*. Asia is already home to half of the world's middle-class population, a demographic that is increasingly eager to exercise its spending power.

So, why not Mongolia next?

The elements for its success are clearly there: a wealth of subsoil resources such as copper, gold, and rare earth metals; a growing number of cutting-edge tech and lifestyle brands; an educated population (Mongolians are consistently among the world's top students in mathematics competitions); and enviable diplomatic relations with countries both in its immediate vicinity and around the world. Mongolia's vast steppe landscape lends itself not only to herding and renewable energy production but to tourism and filmmaking. The country also stands firm on its democratic principles, which bodes well for well-ordered, socially inclusive development. If administered well, and if corruption and political nepotism can be rooted out, Mongolia—as this book will show—stands every chance of becoming Asia's next success story.

Observant readers will have noted the recurrence of the word "if" in the previous sentence. The consultancy firm PricewaterhouseCoopers (PwC) stated in its 2022 Doing Business in Mongolia report that "abundant natural resource wealth and agricultural production make Mongolia's population one of the potentially richest countries per capita in the region." The authors were then careful to say that converting this potential into reality requires many critical factors to function in unison.

These conclusions compare with other assessments of Mongolia's economic and political situation contained in reports by development organizations such as The World Bank, The Asian Development Bank, The European Bank for Reconstruction and Development, and the United Nations, as well as other international banking or analyst groups.

Onereport, by the *Harvard International Review*, found that Mongolia is on the "verge of a mining miracle" and could even become as wealthy per capita as Hong Kong and South Korea over the coming decades. The Oyu Tolgoi copper mine in the Gobi Desert—the fourth biggest in the world and a major supplier of what is a key mineral for many renewable energy systems and in the production of electric vehicles—is about to reach full capacity in its operations, an outcome that will bring significant revenues (at least some of which are likely to be reallocated toward developing other megaprojects in the country.) Mineral-rich Mongolia has been called the "wolf economy," and for good reason.

Mongolia's mining sector contributes a vast amount to its economy and exports, but the government is also working toward diversifying the country's economic base and attracting foreign investment in other sectors. As a result, a variety of new opportunities for businesses and investors has emerged, most notably in technology, infrastructure, cashmere production, and renewable energy.

Concurrently, the government has enacted policies to crack down on corruption, introduce greater transparency, and create a more business-friendly environment. Indeed, at the time of writing this book, more than 100 high-ranking politicians and business executives were under investigation in the biggest corruption crackdown in the country's modern history.

According to the UK government's Department for Business and Trade, "Mongolia has more than a goldmine; Mongolia's opportunities in infrastructure, education, finance and green energy are just as alluring." It adds: "From raw materials to city-building, Mongolia's potential is vast, and represents a great opening for British businesses looking to discover—and be a part of—the next success story."

Smart observers know potential when they see it. But of course, Mongolia's success won't come for free and can't be taken for granted. Quite the opposite. It will require great efforts.

In many ways, this book is about everyone in Mongolia who, like Anar and Oyun-Erdene, has a vision for the country's future. It's about the people who are fighting for a better life for the next generation of Mongolians, sometimes against opposition and headwinds, and those who are trying to build stability and solidarity.

Another man with a vision for Mongolia is Gantumur Luvsan-nyam, leader of the country's opposition Democratic Party and a former minister for education and science. He told me in an interview that with greater economic liberalization, allied to investment in education and free-trade zones, Mongolia has the potential to become a giant of science and technology. His ambition is to bring about a "Silicon Steppe."

Different parties may have competing visions, but what is recurrent across the political spectrum—and indeed across many different sections of Mongolian society—is a sense of real possibility. Indeed, over several trips to Mongolia for research, I met many people just as inspiring as the protagonists mentioned. The cast list includes individuals fighting to strengthen the country's democracy, innovators aiming to realize its promise as a hub for renewable energy, tech and lifestyle entrepreneurs who are shaking up traditional industries, people who have left high-flying jobs on Wall Street to return to the country they love and play their part in moving it forward, and a new generation of kids dreaming big dreams of a brighter tomorrow.

Adding to my motivation for writing this book was a sense that they do things differently in Mongolia. I could see that people were exercising their democratic rights to demonstrate outside the government building against corruption, and that both the government and opposition parties were listening and responding to people's demands, not something that would ever happen in neighboring China or Russia. During these events, the prime minister even went out on the street to speak face to face with protesters—a rare sight in almost any country. Mongolia's unique political culture, in addition to its economic and diplomatic prospects (as outlined), make it a compelling story for any Asia watcher. Before deciding to write this book, however, I consulted a German journalist friend in Hong Kong who has traveled to and covered Mongolia for almost two decades. He didn't hesitate: "Mongolia is a fascinating place that definitely deserves more international recognition." Today, I can only agree.

I hope you'll find the book stimulating and thought-provoking and that it will give you an idea of what Mongolia is—and (more importantly) what it might become.

Before we come to that, though, let's hope the drunken miner in Berkh eventually sobered up and was able to find some peace in life.

About the author

Johan Nylander is an award-winning author and Asia correspondent. His work has been published by CNN, Forbes, Sweden's leading business daily *Dagens Industri,* and many other international media outlets.

His most recent book is *The Epic Split – Why 'Made in China' Is Going out of Style*, a report from the frontline of the US-China trade war. He is also the author of *Shenzhen Superstars – How China's Smartest City Is Challenging Silicon Valley*, which became an Amazon bestseller. He is a cowriter of *Shenzhen: China's Southern Powerhouse*, a coffee table–sized book of photos published by Odyssey Books, and the author of an acclaimed management book titled *Simplify* (Förenkla, Liber publishing).

Nylander frequently gives speeches about Asian and Chinese business and tech trends, including geopolitical risks in the region and how to navigate a new world of trade wars and decoupling.

In 2021, he was named a "guardian of free speech" by the Susanne Hobohm Foundation. During the 2008 financial crisis, Nylander was stationed as a foreign correspondent in London. He has an MBA from the University of Gothenburg.

Nylander lives with his family in Hong Kong.

For more about him, and to stay informed about his next book, visit johannylander.asia.

1

Visionaries and peacemakers

Mongolia's "young tigers" are leading the country's battle against corruption, standing up for democratic values, and upholding a long tradition of neighborly diplomacy.

If places could speak, Sükhbaatar Square, at the heart of Ulaanbaatar, would have many tales to tell. For decades, people have gathered here over the warm summer months for picnics and music events. It's been a place for lovers' meetings, for national celebrations, and for violent demonstrations—all shaping the future of individuals, families, and society. Oh, the stories this square could tell.

On a Sunday afternoon in early September, the air still mild and comfortable, wedding parties can be seen lining up to have their photographs taken in front of the Government Palace and the majestic statue of Chinggis Khan (better known in the West as Genghis Khan). Children run and play all around, filling the square with laughter, their parents struggling to keep up. Some visitors are clothed in the traditional *deel*, a loose calf-length tunic often worn by nomadic herders. Others ride around on rented tandems, while local merchants try to flog paintings and souvenirs to tourists. Across the street from where kids in Thrasher and Wu-Tang Clan T-shirts

13

perform flips and ollies on skateboards, elderly men proudly display their military medals, testament to their glory days. On an artificial lawn, groups of teenage boys and girls play volleyball: I count at least a dozen balls in the air at one point; some bounce away and hit other people picnicking nearby, but they're returned with smiles. One can see young couples holding hands, leaning closer in discreet whispers.

Along the edges of the square, food trucks sell ice cream and *khuushuur* (meat dumplings). Some days the square hosts events, ranging from nomadic markets and hip-hop concerts to a green energy expo and demonstrations of Korean or French gastronomy and culture. But the square's atmosphere—warm and inviting, a microcosm of Mongolian society—is a consistent feature. (At least when the weather allows, that is. Returning in January, when the temperature plummets to as low as minus 40 degrees Celsius and the sky looks like a brown-yellow soup from heavy coal burning, there tends to be a lot fewer picnics.)

Strolling around the square and observing its statues and monuments also offers something of a quick guide to the country's political history.

In the middle of the square stands a statue of Damdin Sükhbaatar, a communist revolutionary. It was somewhere around here that he declared the independence of Mongolia from China in July 1921. The square still bears his name, and the capital itself is named in honor of the "Red Hero" who liberated the country. The words Sükhbaatar pronounced at the moment of independence are engraved on his statue: "If we, the whole people, unite in our common effort and common will, there will be nothing in the world that we cannot achieve, that we will not have learnt or that we will have failed to do." The communist revolution saw the establishment of the Mongolian People's Republic, making Mongolia the first Asian country, and only the second place in the world after Russia, to adopt communism. The regime's close ties to the Red Army allowed Mongolia to fall easily under Russian control, however, and eventually it became a Soviet satellite state. If Sükhbaatar were alive today, he might be pleased to see Mongolia happily independent once again even though it has shaken off communism.

To the west of the government building stands a reminder of the hardships endured under Soviet rule, in the shape of a monument dedicated to the victims of the Kremlin's Great Purge (or Great Terror). During the late 1930s, Soviet leader Joseph Stalin ordered the killing of tens of thousands of Mongols he accused of promoting Tibetan Buddhism or having ties to pro-Japanese spy rings. Buddhist monks made up most of the victims, alongside intellectuals and political dissidents, and their elimination left a deep scar in Mongolia's collective memory. Seizures of private property and forced relocations of nomadic herders also led to widespread unrest—which was brutally crushed. Mass graves containing hundreds of executed monks and civilians were still being discovered as recently as 2003.

Indirectly echoing Sükhbaatar's words about "common effort and common will," the square was also where the first protests were held in 1989 that eventually led to the demise of Soviet rule in Mongolia and steered its transition to parliamentary democracy. Thousands of Mongolians defied a prohibition on demonstrations by gathering in the square to demand freedom and human rights. Banners proclaimed an old Mongolian war cry, "Mongol Brothers and Sisters, to your horses!" Fortuitously, however, those battle cries were not a portent, as the police made no attempt to break up the protests. In fact, there was no bloodshed whatsoever, not even a fistfight or a window smashed.

The political drama didn't end with the fall of communism, though. Right off the southwestern corner of the square, in a tiny park, stands a statue of Sanjaasürengiin Zorig, a prominent Mongolian politician and one of the leaders of the country's democratic revolution. In 1998, he was assassinated—stabbed sixteen times, including three times to the heart. In the days following, mourners crowded Sükhbaatar Square, holding candlelight vigils. The murder is said to have been politically motivated although this has never been proven conclusively. The statue faces the Government Palace, indicating Zorig's morning walk toward his workplace.

In the corner diagonally opposite Sanjaasürengiin you will find a somewhat less disquieting monument. Here, a group of goats balances on a rock, representing the nomadic herder lifestyle and the livestock that yield Mongolia's famous cashmere yarns. Herding is a way of life for over a fifth of Mongolians and defines much about the country's spirit and character. It's probably no coincidence, either, that this goat sculpture is located outside Gobi Cashmere, the city's flashiest cashmere fashion store.

South of the palace stands a symbol—in the shape of an open heart—of Mongolia's important (and often overlooked) role as a regional and global mediator in peace talks and in dialogues for cooperation. It was raised for the 2016 Asia-Europe Meeting, a platform for the two continents to tackle global challenges together. Being a neutral country with strong diplomatic relations both across the entire region and with "third neighbors" such as the US and the EU, Mongolia has been referred to as "the Switzerland of Asia." (Ulaanbaatar was shortlisted to host the 2018 talks between former US President Donald Trump and North Korea's leader, Kim Jong Un, for example, and Mongolia has hosted leaders from both countries.) The inside walls of the monument are full of graffiti tags and scribbles, messages ranging from political slogans and general pro-fanities to "xxx loves yyy 4-ever." Diplomacy in a nutshell.

Overlooking all of this, and poised on a throne atop the stairs of the Government Palace, officially the Parliament House, sits the mighty Chinggis Khan himself—the first Great Khan of the Mongol Empire of the 13th and 14th centuries, the largest contiguous empire in history. The realm expanded to cover most of Eurasia, from the Sea of Japan to parts of Eastern Europe, thanks to its advanced military technology, clever diplomacy, and a massive horde of nomadic warriors. In just 25 years, the Mongol army conquered more lands and people than the Romans subjugated in 400 years.

By the emperor's side sits his son Ögedei and grandson Kublai and his loyal warriors Boruchu and Mukhlai. Both the Chinggis Khan statue and the Government Palace, incidentally, face south, in keeping with the custom of the nomads, who always keep the openings to their tents, or *gers,* oriented toward the sun and away from the chill north winds.

And yet another historical giant—an outside witness to the empire's greatness perhaps—can be discovered in a small park by the square's southeast corner. Here, Marco Polo—the Venetian merchant who journeyed across Asia at the height of the Mongol Empire and who spent two decades in the service of another of history's great rulers, Kublai Khan—is rendered in stone. Polo's stories, passed down for posterity by his biographer, offer unparalleled insight into the cultures and societies that existed along what became known as the Silk Road and into the wonders achieved with the immense wealth created by the civilizations of the East. On Polo's shoulder in Ulaanbaatar sits a falcon, the national bird of Mongolia and a symbol of power and freedom in various cultures.

By way of contrast, all around these monuments to history arises a new modern Mongolia. Glittering skyscrapers—with logos representing the worlds of international hotel groups and finance, alongside those of local banks and energy companies—reach for the sky. The city's shopping malls and hotel complexes are packed with the usual suspects, from Dolce & Gabbana and Rolex to Adidas and Columbia, all vying for your attention (and your credit card) with high-end international restaurants and hipster cafés. Around the next corner you'll find a swinging jazz joint or a decadent nightclub.

The Blue Sky Hotel and Tower, a shark fin-shaped skyscraper designed in imitation of a similar tower in Dubai, is, next to the Government Palace, the city's most iconic building (and indeed the two face each other from opposite ends of Sükhbaatar Square). You could, in fact, mistake much of central Mongolia for many other modern metropolises—but for the fact that its glistening modern buildings stand side by side with older, Soviet-era edifices such as the Cultural Palace and the State Department Store, and with ordinary residential buildings from the communist period too, many of them still bearing signage in Cyrillic script from that time. And if you were to drive to the outskirts of the city, you'd come across yet another component of its built environment: the so-called *Ger* district, a patchwork of slum-like neighborhoods that house most of the city's underprivileged population.

There's one more aspect to Sükhbaatar Square that we haven't mentioned, however, and possibly the most important at that. This is the kind of square that truly acts as a public forum, giving people a voice. Just as it was the venue for the protests against communism in 1989, large (and occasionally violent) demonstrations have been held here regularly in the decades since—often against the government or in remonstration against the country's state of affairs in general. The square is a platform for democracy, and the political focal point of the city.

In December 2022, thousands of protesters descended on it, in temperatures well below freezing, to denounce corruption after high-ranking individuals within the government had been exposed for effectively stealing hundreds of thousands of tons of coal and selling it on the quiet to China, in a racket whose perpetrators have come to be known as the Coal Mafia. (More about this later.) The protesters put pressure on Prime Minister Oyun-Erdene Luvsan-namsrai to name and punish the guilty and to do more to root out corruption. The scandal also fueled bitterness over surging living costs and inequality in the country that had already sparked pro-tests earlier in year, including demands for the government and the premier to simply "do your job!"

Funnily enough, Oyun-Erdene had himself risen to national fame during similar anti-corruption protests some years before his political career really took off. As a grassroots activist, he organized and led multiple mass demonstrations against corruption, most notably one held in 2018 that involved more than 30,000 citizens. At the heart of those demonstrations (and more recent ones) lay a frustration that, in a mineral-rich, democratic country like Mon-golia, many people are still mired in poverty. Oyun-Erdene and his followers demanded transparency, political representation for the young, and radical reforms geared toward social equality. And of course, Sükhbaatar Square was the epicenter of their protests.

When I sit down with Oyun-Erdene during one of several inter-views at the Government Palace, one of my main questions is about just this: How does it feel to have gone from being the one leading mass protests outside the building, and from demanding reforms and resignations from the government of the day, to now being the one inside the building at whom fingers are being pointed and anger directed?

Instead of being taken aback by the question, he lights up.

"Oh, the demonstrators on the square—they are my best advocates," he says. "They are fighters for democracy and quality. Even if we don't agree on everything, and even if we sometimes fail in communication and understanding, we all want the best for the country. The young people are the voice of the future who one day will govern this country."

If Sükhbaatar Square could speak, it would indeed have many stories to tell. One of these would be about the fight for liberty, equality, and democracy.

An oasis of (crippled) democracy

Mongolia is a young democracy. Compared to many other countries that were under the thumb of Soviet dictatorship, however—or whose people have broken away from authoritarian regimes elsewhere in the world—it has made rather a success of standing up for democratic principles and is also often hailed as an inspiration to other societies fighting for egalitarianism. Three decades after Mongolia's first free and democratic election, following the peaceful revolution of 1989, and despite its challenging geographic location—the country is landlocked between the world's two biggest authoritarian states, Russia and China—political and civil rights, as well as a fairly robust parliamentary system, have thrived here, according to international observers.

A 2021 nationwide poll in Mongolia by the International Republican Institute (IRI), a Washington-based non-profit organization, showed strong enthusiasm for democratic governance. When asked about the best possible form of government, 72 percent of Mongolians said they preferred democracy—although most acknowledged the need for continued improvement. Women were in general more optimistic about the country's democratic development than were men, as were the young compared to older generations.

"While many people believe that democracy is backsliding around the world, the people of Mongolia are showing strong support for an open and transparent political system," said Johanna Kao, regional director of the organization's Asia-Pacific division. "It's encouraging to see a thirst for democracy in a country that borders both China and Russia."

Compared with many post-communist Central Asian countries, and even some Eastern European countries—most notably Russia—Mongolia's public is among the least nostalgic about the communist years. According to the Sant Maral Foundation, an independent polling organization, around 90 percent of Mongolians in surveys up until 2007 said "yes" when asked whether they supported the country's transition to a democratic system, and some 80 percent said they supported its transition to a market economy. A later study, in 2022, showed support for democracy holding up: 80 percent of polled Mongolians supported having a system of government involving democratically elected representatives. As the human rights activist and former parliamentarian Oyungerel Tsedevdamba put things in a 2016 speech, almost every household in Mongolia favors the nation's choice of a democratic system.

Countless international observers have offered similar assessments to endorse the view that this mining and herding nation has embraced democratic values over the last three decades and that its people are determined to shun the traps of authoritarian populism to which others in the region have succumbed.

"The challenges are great but so are the opportunities," the UN's resident coordinator in Ulaanbaatar, Tapan Mishra, tells me during an interview in his office. "Mongolia's democracy has the potential to become even stronger."

Former US Secretary of State John Kerry went as far as to describe the Asian nation as an "oasis of democracy" and touted it as an inspirational story of democratic transition.

"You really set a great example," he told Mongolian and American embassy staff at the US ambassador's residence during a visit to Ulaanbaatar in 2016. "You've got China on one side of you, and Russia on the other side of you, and there are always a lot of pressures, and here you are in this oasis of democracy fighting for your own identity."

For his part, Sebastian Surun, the French ambassador to Mongolia, recently said that the two countries "share understanding of the importance of freedom, open society, and democratic rule," and that "Mongolia's democracy delivers."

In "political rights," Mongolia even scored higher than the US, South Korea, and Italy in Freedom House's 2022 rankings. The advocacy group also considered Mongolia a "free" country, in contrast to its "not free" neighbors.

Not bad for a democracy that hasn't even reached middle age.

Speak to people on the streets in Mongolia, however, and you'll get somewhat less of a rosy picture. When I ask Mongolians about the current situation in their country, many say they fear that it's moving in the wrong direction. Some call its democratic and human rights records into question, but concerns over unemployment, healthcare, and the economy are a more constant refrain. Despite having massive natural resources, an educated population, and solid diplomatic relations, the country's GDP per capita has been stuck at around $4,000 for the last decade—which is about the same level as Sri Lanka's currently and half that of Malaysia—and indicates a lack of upward movement for individuals and society. Nearly one in three people live in poverty. What's more, the COVID-19 pandemic left many Mongolians struggling more than ever to make ends meet—inflation topping 15 percent—and according to polls many put the blame on bad local governance rather than global issues such as soaring import prices.

In inequality, Mongolia ranked less unequal than did several wealthy locations including the US and Hong Kong in a 2022 Oxfam report titled "Inequality kills." Many here would probably agree, however, that it does kill. In 2021, life expectancy for Mongolian men was as low as in North Korea and almost ten years lower than in Russia. Mongolia also has the highest rate of liver cancer in the world, and prevalence among women is 16 times higher than the global average, according to a 2017 report by the World Health Organization. When I meet the country's minister of health, Enkhbold Sereejav, I ask him why this is. Without hesitation, he replies: "It's because we drink too much alcohol and eat too much meat."

Screening stations and clinics are being rolled out nationwide, and Enkhbold has launched a campaign to encourage people to go jogging in the morning, but progress will take time. It's also true that bad diet and lack of exercise are just part of the explanation for the country's dreadful statistics. In winter, Ulaanbaatar becomes one of the world's most polluted cities, as a lack of central heating means many households, especially in the poorer parts of town, have to burn coal for heating and cooking—filling the air with toxic pollutants. The city's traffic is often at a standstill, adding to the great winter smog that settles over everything.

Even if an overwhelming majority of Mongolians support democracy, that doesn't mean they are happy with the outcomes it's delivering. In a 2022 poll by the Sant Maral Foundation, more than half of respondents said they were unhappy with the state of things. More worryingly, many felt that politics is characterized mostly by "self-interested politicians and lack of concern for society at large" and functions to "support the rich." Some 85 percent of those polled supported full-scale reforms to fix the sociopolitical-economic system. (I even met a politician, working for the government, who said she generally doesn't trust politicians.)

There's also a widespread feeling that ordinary people are unable to influence political decisions made at the national level. Many observers have expressed concern over a lack of transparency in legislative, executive, and judicial processes, which ultimately undermines both government efficiency and public confidence—and enables corruption. Moreover, the IRI poll highlighted a gap in communication between the government and the governed. When asked what activities ordinary people can use to influence the decisions of politicians, about a third of those aged 18-35 said the best way was not to direct dialogue with the country's leadership but to protest on the streets. Only 6 percent said "Talk with officials," and a paltry 1 percent said "Join a political party."

Still, while few feel listened to by the government, people are in general quick to comment on current affairs and will openly criticize the country's leadership. In my experience, this differentiates Mongolians from people in China, say, or Singapore, or other less open societies. Here, people have opinions on everything and are not afraid to express them. (Foreigners living here tell me that while Mongolians are quick to criticize, they're slower in coming forward with constructive ideas on how to make things better, that too often it starts and ends with grouching. But, hey, that's perhaps a global phenomenon.)

Ahead of my first meeting with the prime minister, and to get a feeling for the sentiment on the streets, I asked a variety of people what they thought I should raise with him. Most did not hold back.

"When you speak with the prime minister, ask him why we are still so poor when we have such a huge land full of resources," a boy in his late teens told me as he puffed on a cigarette outside a bar with a group of friends, "Ask him to tell the truth—the brutal truth."

A man in his late 50s said: "Tell him that we are ready for change, that we are ready for real democracy. I've been ready for 30 years. What are we still waiting for?!"

Another man, who happens to be one of the country's wealthiest and most influential entrepreneurs, and who invited me to dine with him at the swanky country club he owns, demanded: "Ask the PM how to cut dependency on Russia. If we don't, we'll never be free."

A political blogger I met with was less circumspect. "I don't like him; I don't trust any politician," the blogger said, before muttering: "His long-term vision is correct. . . if he can pull it off."

I spoke with opposition politicians, activists, and social workers, who all expressed frustration at the country's levels of inequality and corruption, some even articulating fear that democracy could be eroded if the situation doesn't improve.

However, the biggest critic I encountered of Mongolia's political system and society might well be the prime minister himself. In one of our interviews, he calls Mongolia a "crippled democracy": a country plagued by the disparity between its rich and its poor and by the absence of a substantial middle class; a country beset by political populism and corruption, as well as by the lack of a unifying sense of national identity or any widespread hope for a better future.

"The poor people hate the rich," he says bluntly, with a touch of melancholy, from behind his office desk, observed from the wall by a portrait of his great predecessor as leader, the redoubtable Chinggis Khan. "And society is divided very much because of this disparity. If we have disparity, we will have turmoil in society."

I've interviewed numerous prime ministers, presidents, and ministers in my career but never one so critical of his own country's political system, or indeed of his own party (the Mongolian People's Party, or MPP). Politicians typically paint a rosy picture of their own achievements and blame any failures on the opposition, hiding behind vague excuses. Oyun-Erdene, instead, begins with self-criticism and by outlining the shortcomings of his party. No whitewashing. It's almost as though he must have overheard the plea from the teenage boy I spoke to outside the restaurant: tell the brutal truth.

Then again, Oyun-Erdene is not your ordinary politician.

Chess and a wooden hut

Born in 1980, Oyun-Erdene was only 38 years old when he became secretary of the cabinet of the Mongolian government and 40 when he became Mongolia's prime minister, making him one of the youngest national leaders in the world. He had grown up with his maternal grandparents—a renowned Buddhist abbot, candidate chess master, and school instructor in both mathematics and the Mongolian language—in the working-class town of Berkh, in Khentii province. It was an upbringing very different from that experienced by those born into the capital's social and political elites.

However, having a scholastic upbringing undoubtedly brought him advantages. Oyun-Erdene shone academically, ultimately earning degrees in journalism and law from the National University of Mongolia, and later in one in public policy from the Kennedy School of Government at Harvard University. His Ivy League schooling marks him out from a previous generation of leaders often educated in the former Soviet bloc.

At the age of 21, he ran the governor's office in Berkh. Later, he worked locally, as well as overseas, for World Vision, a Christian humanitarian organization that aims to create lasting change in the lives of children, families, and communities living in poverty. It was an experience that left him painfully aware of the development problems his country faced. Oyun-Erdene has written of feeling "saddened to see how bureaucratic, corrupt, and politically divided" Mongolia had become in comparison with much of the rest of the world, and frustrated at how opportunities were being squandered due to the "irresponsible and unethical actions" of civil servants.

"I think this sadness and frustration both influenced me to become a politician," he said in a 2021 interview published on the Kennedy School's website.

His career as a social activist, however, began much earlier, at around the age of nine. Oyun-Erdene had a speech impediment as a child and didn't say his first words until he was five years old, when, the story goes, he announced it was raining outside, a pronouncement that was deemed to be auspicious, given the country's routine water shortages. Despite his verbal hindrance, he was a vocal boy in his own way. In primary school he wrote a poem about his school's cleaning lady, whom he had observed struggling to keep the floors clean with a mop and bucket while students and teachers walked over them in muddy boots without any acknowledgement of her efforts. The poem was published in the school paper, and the cleaning lady broke down in tears when she read it. Someone had noticed her! On another occasion, Oyun-Erdene took to the stage during a parents' day—an unexpected move for the school's administration—and read out a poem to the assembled parents and teachers about abusive fathers and alcohol. "That child is strange," some of the adults whispered.

Much of his political consciousness came from his grandfather, who, along with his grandmother, raised him after his parents divorced, and from whom he adopted the patronymic Luvsannamsrai. They lived in a one-room wooden hut with a small garden in the outskirts of Berkh, every inch a mining town. In the middle of the room stood a small stove for heating and cooking, and there were two beds on opposite sides of the room.

A tree the family planted together in Oyun-Erdene's childhood now stands tall, with sturdy branches, decades later. The current inhabitant of the house, a young man named Gan-Erdene, told me when I visited that it was slightly surreal to know that the prime minister of his country had once lived in these same humble quarters.

Simple though it may look, this house was the venue for many long conversations between grandfather and grandson on such topics as philosophy, Buddhism, and literature, as well as for endless hours of chess games. This formed Oyun-Erdene and laid the foundation of a curiosity that persists to this day. I also had the pleasure of meeting his former primary school teacher, Togoon Tumur, a sweet lady with attentive eyes and cheeks shaped like peaches, who said that her former student would challenge her by asking questions—about anything and everything.

"I had to go home and do research, and the next day he would sit there, impatiently, awaiting the answer," she told me, her eyes twinkling from the memory. "It was not always easy." Some of

Oyun-Erdene's childhood friends told me similar stories although they usually had far less patience with his endless queries.

By chance I also ran into a close friend of Oyun-Erdene's grand-father, Erdene-Ochir, a chess master and former head of the local chess club. He explained how he and Luvsannamsrai senior, almost 30 years apart in age, would spend long hours playing chess and talking about life, politics, and education, occasionally over a few vodkas. Luvsannamsrai was the principal of a local school at the time—and had his own philosophy of schooling.

"He was a natural educator, but he could be tough," said Erdene-Ochir, wearing a baseball cap and a heavy ring inscribed with the Buddhist swastika. "He would require the children in school to maintain principles and to be disciplined and consistent in their actions. He wanted them to learn to follow what they had set out to do, live up to what they had promised, and to keep their word. He didn't like people quitting easily. This was true for the upbringing of Oyun-Erdene, too."

He added: "I believe that growing up in this working-class town, where mining was the backbone of the economy, added to people's characteristics. Everybody had respect for the workers. Also, you had many women operating heavy machinery. That was the culture of Berkh."

Erdene-Ochir told me that the prime minister and his late grand-father had one particular thing in common: their style of playing chess. They shared a sensitive and pragmatic approach to the game. Even when implementing a clear strategy, for example, they would not hesitate to adapt to a changing situation on the board. A common mistake in chess, he explained, is to be too stubborn. He added that the prime minister, whom he played several times, had a knack for some classic "trapping" methods (whereby a player tries to lure an opponent into playing a move that results in the opponent's own disadvantage) and the tactic of "removing a defender," where the objective is to drive away a guarding piece so as to take advantage of an opponent's resulting positional weakness and prevent risk to one's own guard.

"Last time I met the PM, some years ago, he told me that he was applying chess thinking and techniques in real life and in politics," the chess master said with a smile. "I was not surprised."

His grandfather comes up often in my conversations with Oyun-Erdene, and indeed when I talk with other people about the prime minister. On one occasion, I ask him to name his main political influences, or the people in history from whom he has drawn lessons about leading. It came as no surprise that he immediately named his grandfather. In conversation, he frequently refers to things he learned from his grandfather, and people close to him confirm that he often weighs decisions or opinions against what his grandfather would have done or thought.

Next to his grandfather, Oyun-Erdene mentions two political lodestars: Deng Xiaoping and Nelson Mandela. Both need a little explaining.

As the de facto leader of China after Mao Zedong, Deng Xiaoping was the main architect of the country's reform and opening-up policies that began to be enacted in the late 1970s. An advocate of economic pragmatism, he minted various aphorisms such as: "Seek truth from facts," and "Black cat or white cat, if it can catch mice, it's a good cat." In my 2017 book, *Shenzhen Superstars – How China's Smartest City Is Challenging Silicon Valley*, I tried to explain Deng's view on the importance of no-nonsense economic reforms: "Deng disagreed with other politicians in China who said that the flow of refugees into Hong Kong—many of whom risked their lives to swim across Shenzhen Bay—was a public security issue that should be dealt with by clamping down and policing the border. The basic problem, Deng argued, was economics. The economy on the Chinese side of the border had fallen too far behind and it was understandable that young people should flee to Hong Kong where they were promised opportunities for a better way of life. The answer, he said, was in economic development on the Chinese side of the border." Today, many Mongolians are leaving the country to seek better economic opportunities elsewhere. The answer, if we paraphrase from Deng, is in economic development in Mongolia.

If pragmatism is what Oyun-Erdene learned from Deng, Nelson Mandela offers a different kind of example—that of never compromising on your core beliefs. The South African anti-apartheid and democracy activist, and later president and Nobel Peace Prize laureate, served 27 years behind bars as a political prisoner, but he never lowered his head to his oppressors. He said: "A winner is a dreamer who never gives up." Mandela never wavered in his devotion to democracy, equality, and education. He was also, incidentally, a keen chess player and "calculated every move as he does in politics," according to one of his closest confidants.

As alluded to, working for World Vision throughout much of his 20s—during which time Oyun-Erdene became a regular visitor to the capital for meetings—was also formative for the future leader. When he joined the organization, he had just graduated from university, and "his world view and philosophy were just being established," according to Batbaatar Bayangerel, who hired him and served as his boss and mentor for many years.

"When I interviewed him [for the job as regional manager], he was honest and said: 'I want to improve myself, I want to challenge myself, I want to improve my English, I'd like to understand [things better]," Batbaatar Bayangerel tells me when we meet in Ulaanbaatar. "He was humble but straightforward. There were a lot of competitors for this position, with well-experienced people competing for the job, but I saw that [he had a] good heart, and I trusted him."

"He had grown up in the countryside and had seen the inequalities between different groups of society; he had seen the injustice. Remember, at that time Mongolia was just out of being a communist regime and transitioning into a new society. The changes were happening everywhere but in an unequal way."

Batbaatar, educated in linguistic theory and holding a PhD in public policy from the University of Miami, today serves as an advisor to the prime minister and was one of the main authors of the Vision 2050 roadmap. "The roles were switched; he's now my boss," he says with a modest smile, and it's plain to perceive the strong bonds that exist between the two men, forged over many years of working closely together.

The thrust of their work with World Vision was about empowering local communities, improving participation rates in education, boosting livelihoods and resilience, and increasing access to water and sanitation. All communities have their own problems, Batbaatar says, and all communities need their own solutions. To make any plan work, he adds, local people must be involved collectively in shaping and achieving those solutions. Over the years Batbaatar and Oyun-Erdene helped thousands of children, whether through offering shelter and safety from abusive parents, helping them to study, or simply giving them space to express their concerns and discover their identities. They also helped teachers to improve their teaching methods and herders to understand more about the business side of agriculture and how to diversify their incomes.

Much of the thinking and techniques they used were based on the ideas of Amartya Sen, an Indian economist and philosopher who was awarded the 1998 Nobel Prize in Economic Sciences for his contributions to welfare and development economics and for his interest in the problems of society's poorest members. Sen, today a professor of economics and philosophy at Harvard, has asserted that development cannot be measured only by economic growth because it also requires establishing the basis for people to live rewarding and happy lives. Social arrangements, Sen proposed, should be evaluated according to the extent to which they give people the freedom to acquire capabilities that add value to their lives and improve their well-being. Inspired by Sen, the World Vision team took the approach of supporting rural people to set up their own vehicles—so-called community-based organizations (CBOs)—to drive improvements at a local level. It also, crucially, helped these organizations to connect with one another.

"Once we had many different CBOs, they started to create alliances," says Batbaatar. "One of the purposes with community organizing is to gain power. Now, these groups could start forming collaborations—and gain more power. As individuals they are powerless, but when they join together they are powerful. They get empowered, they can take action. They could now challenge governors and corrupt people."

Remember the story of Alan Gua, about solidarity and unity: *"If you are on your own, you will break easily. But when you are together, you are unbreakable."*

Strategies and grandiose ideas, as everyone knows, can be miles apart from reality. During a visit to World Vision's headquarters in Khentii province I was shown around its offices and workshop spaces and heard all about its mission and its projects. But it wasn't until I went outside, to view the garden, that I got a real—and startling—idea of its day-to-day purpose. A door stood open at the back of the building, and I looked in. There, on a bunkbed, I saw a young teenage girl asleep with her back to me, her hair dark on the white sheets. I was told that she was one of many girls who had run away from home and sought shelter here.

This image of the girl has stayed with me. It's hard not to think about what abuses she might have been exposed to or what awaited her once she left the safehouse. But whatever horrors she was running from, at least for a while she could sleep in safety.

Batbaatar explains how Oyun-Erdene went from being "a true grassroots worker" to entering the political world; how over the years he rose to fame in the capital, became a member of parliament, organized large-scale anti-corruption demonstrations outside the government building—and eventually helmed the party and the country. When I ask if he was ever surprised about his former protégé becoming prime minister, he tells me a story from one of their earliest encounters. During a workshop, the new recruits for World Vision were given an assignment to sit and draw a number of specific objects, however interpretively they liked. Oyun-Erdene just drew a big sun in the middle of the page, and inside he placed a house, a family, a river, and so on. He said: "The sun is hope; the hope of the sun is my vision."

"When he became PM, that came to my mind. He was a young kid at that time but had this vision. I felt like now the sun has risen," says Batbaatar with more than a little sentimentality in his voice.

Yes, this particular sun has risen. But today many dark clouds dim Mongolia's skies—and the sunlight of democracy and anti-corruption are threatened by powerful elements trying to put it to bed.

Three stones and a long-term vision

To describe the way he sees society—and more importantly, how to fix its problems—Oyun-Erdene has an analogy about making tea. In the countryside, a traditional way of making tea is to balance the teapot over a fire on three stones. If all three stones are strong and of equal size, the pot will be stable. If any of the stones is smaller or weaker than the others, it will collapse. The same goes for society, he explains. And the three stones—or pillars—of Oyun-Erdene's society, are individual freedom, economic strength, and the rule of law.

"In Mongolia, we have individual freedom," he says. "That's solid. But we don't have strong enough economic freedom or economic strengths. And we have flawed rule of law. The three stones are not even, and there's a risk of collapse."

(The same principle may well be as true for individual families as it is for whole societies. One might recollect the first sentence of Leo Tolstoy's novel *Anna Karenina*: "Happy families are all alike; every unhappy family is unhappy in its own way." For a family to be happy, Tolstoy means, it's necessary to have three things in reasonable measure: the health of family members, financial security, and mutual affection. If there is a deficiency in any one or more of these key aspects, the family will be unhappy. The teapot will collapse.)

Oyun-Erdene's voice is soft but determined and confident. He speaks like a visionary pragmatist. There is no revolutionary vocabulary, no promises of quick fixes. People close to him say he could benefit from being more vocal, more "salesman like" when it comes to his political plans. The prime minister doesn't agree: he believes that actions speak louder than words. He wants people to judge him for his accomplishments and for tangible improvements in their lives rather than on his rhetoric. On a similar note, he says it's of lesser importance for him to be credited for those accomplishments.

"What's important is that people receive the benefit of the change, and that they feel the change," he says. "The most important thing is that we have the advancement, we have the performance, that people are benefiting in real life. It's not important who gets the credit. Personal glory is always in vain."

He adds: "Only after people receive the benefits of GDP growing, after [it affects] their day-to-day life, only then will they recognize me as a true leader. I won't be remembered for attending many opening ceremonies or ribbon cutting; that's not important."

The vision, or long-term goal, of the prime minister, and of his government, is to make the stones of society strong and even. The key elements of his plan involve rooting out corruption and political populism, diversifying the economy in a way that allows various sectors to climb the value chain, and fostering a common national identity that paves the way for a new generation of patriotic and humane leaders. If all goes to plan, his reforms will bring into being a stable society with a sizable middle class.

One of the basic theories of democracy, put forth by Aristotle millennia ago, concerns its causal link to the existence of a thriving middle class. According to the Greek philosopher, a large, prosperous middle class can mediate between rich and poor, creating the structural foundations upon which democratic political processes may flourish. "When there is no middle class, and the poor greatly exceed in number, troubles arise, and the state soon comes to an end," he wrote.

Beyond Aristotelian theory, the specifically commercial role of the middle class has also been demonstrated across different societies in history, and its economic advance is generally seen as a bringer of democratic institutions, the rule of law, and limits on executive power. In a country such as Mongolia, where mining dominates everything, the status quo—in which a small elite wields dominance over a large base of poor workers—can almost seem like the natural order. Only through the establishment and growth of a healthy middle class, goes the theory, can this order be broken and democratic rule consolidated. For society to be successful, Oyun-Erdene believes, at least 70 percent of people should be middle class.

"If a society doesn't have a major proportion of middle-class people, then democracy won't work," he says. "Therefore, one of the main concepts of Vision 2050 is to focus on the middle class. We want to expand the middle class in this society."

The government's Vision 2050 roadmap, the nation's first long-term development strategy, was developed by Oyun-Erdene when he was cabinet secretary under his predecessor as prime minister, Ukhnaagiin Khürelsükh (today the country's president), and approved by parliament in May 2020. Ultimately, its aim is to transform the country into a leading regional power through (among other things) reducing poverty, creating a greener economy, improving education, and advancing gender equality in the job market. Put simply, it hopes to redefine Mongolian society.

The "vision" sets out nine fundamental goals, covering human development, governance, "a peaceful and safe society," green growth, shared national values, quality of life, growing the middle class, regional development, and "people-centered cities." It also lays down 50 specific objectives to be achieved in the medium to long term. And all of this goes hand in hand with the administration's so-called New Recovery Policy, a 10-year development plan to encourage Mongolia's post-pandemic recovery by opening it up to domestic and foreign investment. By promoting six economic drivers that are currently deemed to be lacking—trade ports, energy diversification, industrialization, urban and rural development, green development, and efficient governance—the recovery plan aims to increase industrial output and mitigate the vulnerabilities that come with being a land-locked territory.

I meet several people in Mongolia who are critical of the administration's plans: they complain, variously, that they're too vague or too detailed, too state-focused or too dominated by private interests, too ambitious or not ambitious enough. But almost everyone—including opposition politicians—agrees on one thing: the country is in desperate need of some kind of long-term strategy to improve its governance and economic standing in ways that enable it to achieve its full potential. It's been 33 years since democratization began; now the government wants to turn the page and look ahead at the three decades to come. As the collapse of communism recedes in the rearview mirror, there is a widespread sense that Mongolia is at another turning point.

"If Mongolia succeeds and attains all of its Vision 2050 goals, this will involve a significant transformation of the country for the next decades," writes the European Institute for Asian Studies (EIAS), a think tank based in Brussels. "For the first time, it seems possible to imagine a shift in the Mongolian dependence on raw coal, not only because of its aspiration towards facilitating green growth but also because of its aim to turn its cities, especially its capital, into eco-friendly and smart cities. Fighting the exodus from the rural areas to the cities will necessarily lead to the development of its most remote and rural areas while strengthening the middle class."

In monetary terms, the government aims to increase GDP per capita tenfold: from $4,000 in 2020 to almost $40,000 by the middle of the century. That's about the same GDP per capita as Japan enjoys today.

This aspiration might seem particularly bold, but it's perhaps not unrealistic when you consider that Mongolia's economy grew tenfold in the 25 years following the 1990 transition to democracy. Country managers of international development banks who I speak to all say the goal is within reach, especially considering the relatively modest starting point and the country's small population size. In the government's number crunching, three different calculations were used to model economic growth, and a target somewhere in the middle was selected as the official aspiration.

José Luis Diaz Sanchez, the World Bank's senior country economist for Mongolia, is among those who believe the GDP target is "very ambitious" but "possible." The bank predicts Mongolia's economy will expand annually by somewhere around 6 to 7 percent in 2024 and 2025, and probably in the following years too, as foreign reserves and overall revenues boom from mining exports. But more important than economic expansion is the quality of that expansion. During an interview at the World Bank's office in Ulaanbaatar, Diaz Sanchez repeatedly highlights the need for Mongolia to diversify its economy away from mining. As long as it remains dependent on revenues from a handful of commodities, the country and its people will be at the mercy of fluctuating global commodity prices and of the boom-and-bust cycles that go along with them. That's not sustainable (more about this in Chapter 2). Diaz Sanchez also notes that increased GDP isn't worth a massive amount if it doesn't correlate with upward social mobility among a country's population at large.

His words are echoed by several other development specialists.

"The economic goals are definitely realistic and within reach. Mongolia is not only the country of eternal blue sky but also a country of eternal opportunities," chimes Hannes Takacs, head of the European Bank for Reconstruction and Development (EBRD) in Mongolia, although he also highlights the need for political stability and further progress against corruption to make the most of these opportunities.

In agreement with the World Bank, EBRD, which provides project financing mainly for private enterprises in democratic countries, sees Mongolia's GDP growing at around 7 percent annually over the coming years, largely due to increased mining activity but also tourism.

Boosting the economy and GDP per capita will, the government hopes, tilt the momentum toward the creation of a permanent middle class that enjoys a good standard of living. Family incomes are to be increased, sustainably, by promoting employment and by creating the right conditions for competitive micro-, small-, and medium-sized businesses to thrive.

Gantumur Luvsannyam, leader of the country's opposition Democratic Party, also has a positive outlook on the economy but believes the current administration's policies are holding Mongolia's potential back. In an interview at its headquarters, close to the Government Palace, Gantumur tells me his party's ambitions are clear: to build a capitalistic society based on economic freedom and human rights. Today, he says, there's too much state interference in the business sector.

"The share of state-owned businesses and commerce plays a huge role here," he says. "Our core message is that we want to increase the share of the private sector and diminish state interference."

To increase economic freedom, he adds, the Democratic Party wants to lower taxes, get rid of red tape and bureaucracy, and diminish the old burdens of state control. This would in turn add oil to economic growth and attract foreign direct investments (FDI).

"There's so many areas of opportunities to invest and grow in Mongolia," Gantumur says. "What's hindering this is all the state bureaucracy. Our view is that our economy must grow two times in a very short term—not in the distant 2050 future. To achieve that, all sectors must be liberalized, and Mongolia must have a more business-friendly environment. Once we've achieved that, we can meet all those great growth numbers."

Mongolia has been referred to as "the wolf economy." The term was reportedly coined by Ganhuyag Chuluun Hutagt, a renowned entrepreneur and former vice minister of finance, and was subsequently put in circulation overseas by Renaissance Capital, a London-based frontier markets-focused investment bank, in a 2009 report in which the authors said: "We think Mongolia may be able to position itself as the next Asian tiger, or, as they prefer, Mongolian wolf."

The wolf is revered in Mongolia. It's a potent symbol of Mongolian identity and nationhood. An ancient legend has it that the Mongols are descendants of a mythical blue wolf, and some regard wolves as heavenly. The name "Blue Wolf" also reflects the Mongolian origins of the name Chinggis. Seeing a wolf conveys good luck, boosting a person's *hiimori*, or energy.

Oyun-Erdene, however, prefers to think of the country in relation to another national symbol, the horse, and in particular the "wind" (and winged) horse that features on the Mongolian state emblem. Mongolia is indeed known as the land of the horse, and Mongols have a reputation for being the best horse riders on the planet. Horses also have strong historical symbolism. As Paige Williams, an American journalist, has written: "Chinggis Khan would not have been Chinggis Khan without the everyday Mongolian horse. In the 13th century, his Mongol Empire conquered half of Asia and Eastern Europe on horseback." It's been said that a Mongol without a horse is like a bird without wings.

The "wind horse" represents speed and symbolizes Mongolia's independence and sovereign spirit. More generally, horses represent friendship and loyalty, according to Oyun-Erdene.

"Mongolia will become the stallion of Asia," he tells me. "More than a 'wolf economy,' Mongolia can be one of the leading countries in Asia in terms of competitive advantage and social development. It's more than economics; it's about who we are."

"The stallion represents Mongolian identity, a person of good nature," he adds, pointing to the wind horse on the state emblem on the wall behind him.

Almost 1,500 specialists, ranging across many different disciplines and academic backgrounds, helped to create Vision 2050. They were all Mongolians, but they did consult analysts from different countries and organizations and followed policy examples from Singapore, Estonia, and other developed nations. It took two years to finalize the plan, and the first draft was more than 600 pages long, according to Batbaatar. There were, inevitably, tensions and disagreements over which mathematical models or scientific methods to use, and arguments between, for example, environmental exponents and mining representatives. But the approach was inclusive and always geared toward negotiation and compromise.

Batbaatar explains how Oyun-Erdene first approached him to join the project and outlined his aspirations for it on a whiteboard.

"He said, 'We need to redesign, rethink, revisit, review, re re re ... The last 30 years have been bad. We need change. We need radical reforms," Batbaatar recalls. "Then he asked me, 'Are you ready to do this?' And I said 'yes.'"

Several people interviewed for this book give similar recollections of formal or informal meetings with Oyun-Erdene, in private or in groups, and of how his passion and zest for the future of the country and its people inspired them to get on board with his quest.

For that quest to succeed and for Mongolia to unlock its potential as wolf economy, or stallion nation, several factors need to coalesce and fall into place, and over the next few subchapters we'll look at some of those components of Oyun-Erdene's puzzle: how to empower a new young generation of leaders, how to root out corruption, how to find a common identity for the country, and how to connect it to the wider world.

Empowering the "young tigers"

"Have you heard of the Chicago Boys? We are the Chicago Boys of Mongolia!" says Batnairamdal "Nagi" Otgonshar, a former Wall Street banker who now works under Oyun-Erdene as secretary for foreign affairs, with a smile that stretches from ear to ear.

He's referring to a group of Chilean economists prominent in the 1970s and 1980s, most of whom were educated at the Department of Economics of the University of Chicago under economist Milton Friedman, the 20th century's most prominent advocate of free markets. After they finished their studies in the US and returned home, they took up positions in Chile (and some other South American countries) as government advisers, many of them reaching senior positions. They have been referred to as "the boys who got to remake an economy."

A similar phenomenon is happening in Mongolia although the main characters didn't study in Chicago and are not all "boys." What they have in common with the Latin Americans, though, is that they are Western-educated and have left well-paid or prestigious positions with international companies to move back to their home country and accept government jobs in the hope of creating a better future for Mongolia. It's been described as a "new wave." Many of these Mongolians were persuaded or inspired by Oyun-Erdene himself. During his time at Harvard, the future prime minister had many impassioned discussions with other Mongolian students about how to advance—or "save"—their nation. Several individuals I met remember long and fiery debates with him about Mongolia's future, sometimes in cramped student rooms, sometimes in a pub over drinks, sometimes out walking.

"We gathered and talked about what we can do about Mongolia, how we can develop the nation, and how we can have representatives from a whole generation," Nagi Otgonshar says. "He pushed me to be part of this change."

He wasn't immediately persuaded, though. After graduating from Harvard Business School in 2017, he joined Merrill Lynch Bank of America as an investment banker, working first on mergers and acquisitions in New York and then as a trader in natural resources in Sydney. He was happy to live abroad, and life was good. But the prime minister was persistent, and in the end Nagi Otgonshar moved back to Ulaanbaatar to work as an advisor to the Cabinet when Oyun-Erdene was cabinet secretary, and later as vice minister in the Ministry of Mining and Heavy Industry. Today he is one of the top players within the ruling party.

When asked if going from being a Wall Street banker to a government official meant taking a pay cut, he bursts out laughing. "Oh

God, yes! Compared to before I hardly get paid at all now. If I was a money-driven person I would have stayed at Bank of America; no one in Mongolia can pay as much as they did. [But] my work here is valuable and impactful on a human level."

Sitting on the edge of his seat, his elbow leaning on the table before him, he speaks with great enthusiasm and conviction. Mongolia's economy has the opportunity to leapfrog others, he says. It's standing on the edge of greatness. But it will take large investments in infrastructure and a wholesale modernization of the country's economy and business sector. The time is now, he says.

To explain his desire to help his country, he shows me a short essay he wrote while studying at Harvard Business School. Each year, students are asked a straightforward, simple question taken from the lines of a poem by the Pulitzer Prize-winning author Mary Oliver: "Tell me, what is it you plan to do with your one wild and precious life?" This was Nagi's response:

Another blackout. Another dark evening in Khovd—a small town in western Mongolia. I am eight years old. I whine and complain when I burn my hair on the flame of a candle while doing my homework. Next morning, I cry again while I am forced to walk along with my siblings for two hours to our vegetable plot. . .

As a child, I did not fully understand the economic struggles after the collapse of socialism in Mongolia. After the withdrawal of the Soviets from our country, we often lost electricity, food became scarce, and even my father disappeared in search of work. I did not understand how far my mother had to go out in the snow to buy candles, so that I had the luxury to study at night while others sat in darkness. I did not realize that the only way she could feed us was by walking ten miles to her two-hectare vegetable plot that she watered and tended entirely by hand.

At night, walking through the abundant sparkling lights of the HBS campus, I enjoy the world that my mother could only dream of for her children, the world that every mother dreams of for her child. I will go back to my Mongolia. I will be part of the new generation of leaders who will guide the country towards a productive, sustainable, and prosperous path. I want to rebuild Mongolia, so that no mother will ever have to trudge through the snow again, sacrificing every day to ensure a better future for her children.

Nagi Otgonshar also refers to a book that inspired him to make this important life decision: *How Will You Measure Your Life?* by Harvard Business School Professor Clayton M. Christensen. It's an inspirational read, and a *New York Times* bestseller, about how to pursue purpose and meaning through work and to ask the difficult questions required to find better solutions in your career and your personal life. Professor Christensen writes: "Too many of us who start down the path of compromise will never come back. Considering the fact that you'll likely spend more of your waking hours at your job than in any other part of your life, it's a compromise that will always eat away at you." The book has struck a chord with many business leaders, especially in Christensen's reflections on pursuing fulfillment and on using your talent to benefit society.

"I could relate to this," says Nagi. "So many Harvard graduates are successful in their careers and accumulate a lot of money, but are they really happy? This book showed me that many are not. For me, I was chasing 'the American dream,' to get rich. But this dream is very commercial and materialistic. It doesn't consider values that you can't measure in monetary terms, and those are easily ignored. So when the PM reached out, I was ready."

His comments about purpose and fulfillment remind me of a quote by Jordan Peterson, the Canadian psychologist and author:

"It's a luxury to pursue what makes you happy. It's a moral obligation to do what you find meaningful."

Several people interviewed for this book speak of similar inspiration and desires.

"I had never thought of joining the government," says Uyanga Bold, who holds a PhD from the Department of Earth and Planetary Sciences at Harvard and is today head of the Geology Policy Department at Mongolia's Ministry of Mining and Heavy Industry. "I thought of government jobs as boring and stiff. Now a lot of young people are joining [the government]. It's like a new wave. In a way, that makes us role models for a new generation—and we can't let them down."

Another Harvard alumnus is Solongoo Bayarsaikhan. Before taking up a government position, she had a career in international law. Besides running her own practice in Ulaanbaatar, she spent time as a senior associate at Hogan Lovells, one of the world's top law firms, and as a managing partner of Avinex Partners, a local corporate law firm.

"I had previously no interest in Mongolian politics . . . but I could also see so much inequality in terms of livelihood and education in Mongolia," she tells me in an interview, explaining her call to duty.

Given her background in helping international companies arrange their legal affairs in Mongolia, and the fact that she has a degree in mining law, Oyun-Erdene (when cabinet secretary) approached her with a special request: to lead the government's negotiations with Rio Tinto regarding the Oyu Tolgoi copper mine. She had earlier been appointed as deputy chief of the Cabinet Secretariat, in 2020, and was made vice minister for Justice and Home Affairs in the autumn of 2021.

It's not just in Ulaanbaatar that women are making their way in government, however. Bolormaa Enkhbat, who was previously chief of staff to the current prime minister, is now the country's first ever female regional governor, in Khovd province. Armed with a CV that includes roles at the Asian Infrastructure Investment Bank, the Green Climate Fund, and the World Bank, and a degree in public administration from Columbia University in New York, she has made headlines for her demands that Mongolian decision-makers pay more attention to economic development in smaller towns and rural communities.

In an interview with Britain's *Telegraph* newspaper about how Mongolia was among the quickest nations at rolling out Covid-19 vaccinations, she attributed that success to good diplomatic relations but added: "Mongolians have this very warrior-like spirit. You know, a 'we want to get this done and we're going to get this done' type of attitude." According to people I spoke with, that spirit also defines Bolormaa's personality and commitment to the people of her province and country.

In Chapter 3, we'll also meet Bolor-Erdene Battsengel, an Oxford graduate who is now one of the country's foremost tech personalities. At the age of 29, she became vice minister in the Ministry of Digital Development and Communications, the youngest Mongolian ever to attain such high office.

Over the course of my many travels in Mongolia, I met numerous Mongolians who say they have returned from abroad, or hope to return permanently, to support the nation's development. Something like an inborn sense of connection and responsibility, this narrative is a noticeable part of their social identity. One woman who has lived in the US for some ten years, and who I meet while she is visiting her home country, tells me she has "a hole in her chest," a feeling that she is not contributing enough to her country's development. Because of this, she says, she is considering moving back to Mongolia together with her family.

Weighed against this trend, I should say, many other people I speak to say they plan to leave Mongolia because of a lack of job opportunities and the heavy pollution although several say they would prefer to stay if the situation in the country was better. Moreover, attracting young professionals to government positions—and getting them to stay long-term—is far from easy. A representative for the Democratic Party told me that drives to widen the government's talent pool have been attempted in the past but that many youngsters found it hard to fit into the culture of government institutions and soon left their jobs or even the country.

Today, however, it's notable that the fresh blood coursing through government corridors has not gone unnoticed by academics and media commentators.

Jargalsaikhan Dambadarjaa, founder of Jargal Defacto, a think tank and media company, calls Mongolia's new foreign-educated generation "the Harvard youth" and writes that many Mongolians hope these young leaders can help the country address the problems and challenges facing its public governance, society, and economy.

"Citizens expect that young leaders will lead the effort to exercise good public governance and eradicate corruption, which the Mongolian public sector suffers greatly from and struggles to eliminate," he has written. "The country's development and the quality of people's lives will depend on how and when we manage to transition from state administration to public management. Moreover, young people are tasked with effectively and efficiently introducing remarkable developments in science and technology, such as artificial intelligence, blockchain, electric batteries, and other new technologies in all spheres of economic, social, and political life."

The "new blood," is, of course, not just that of the "Harvard youth" group but younger appointments to the Cabinet in general. Julian Dierkes and Bolor Lkhaajav, two prominent Mongolia scholars, wrote in 2021 that, while changing the culture of the ruling MPP remained a challenge to be confronted, the emergence of a new generation in government was "refreshing." "The appointment of Oyun-Erdene offers the possibility of transformative generational change in Mongolia's leadership," they commented. "The newly elected prime minister represents a younger generation of leaders that have studied abroad, exposed to democratic principles, societies, and policies . . . The country is moving away from political leaders who were primarily trained in the Soviet bloc and its successor states and who have followed party careers or were 'heroes' of the 1990 revolution. The looming economic challenge is now inherited by a younger generation of leaders."

(To clarify Mongolia's political arrangements, the prime minister is the head of government and heads the Cabinet. The president is head of state and has the right to veto legislation and the power to appoint key figures such as supreme court judges. It's a confusing system where power is divided between a president elected by the people and a prime minister elected by parliament, and proposals are under discussion to bring the system more in line with traditional parliamentary republican systems like that of Germany.)

As mentioned, encouraging young people to get involved in organized politics in Mongolia isn't easy; only 1 percent in the IRI poll agree that joining a political party offers the best way to influence the decisions of politicians. Nevertheless, the wave of new people joining the administration has proven inspirational to many young

Mongolians, anecdotally at least. And in a country where almost a third of the population is below the age of 34, young people are a force to be taken seriously.

Aubrey Menard wrote in her 2020 book, *Young Mongols,* that "while Mongolia's land is rich with natural resources, its greatest resource is its young people."

In this context, Oyun-Erdene wants to take on the role of bridge builder. He sees himself as a link between two generations: those who grew up in Soviet times, and those who have only known democracy. He also tells me that he sometimes thinks of himself as a comma—","—between the last 30 years and the 30 to come, between the old and the young essentially.

"We have to empower the young people," he says. "In order to truly create a powerful nation, we need the youth in politics. That's why we're encouraging the young generations to take up decision-maker roles as vice ministers and ministers. So, young blood, new blood."

Half jokingly, he refers to these young recruits as "young tigers" who are still sharpening their teeth in the political world, his own task being to keep them safe and guide them forward. As you have probably realized by now, Oyun-Erdene often uses national symbols or tales from nature to make a point. In thinking about his role as a leader to the young, he offers another story that his grandfather told him about birds. When migrant, or nomadic, birds fly to a new destination, legend has it there's always one bird out in front who leads the flock: the leader bird. (In reality, the birds take turns at leading, but the story is what matters here.) This bird is the first to face the wind and the weather and takes responsibility for making sure the group lands safely at its new destination. Buffeted and damaged by the wind, however, it dies on arrival, its job done. Oyun-Erdene sees himself in this vein. He knows that his role as leader will come to an end at some point in the future, but when it does he wants to have conveyed the country to a new place and with a new generation of qualified, patriotic leaders ready to run things for themselves.

"I'll keep flying until my time is over," he says. "I'll keep protecting the 'young tigers' until they're fully grown up and able to defend themselves. Mongolia needs leaders who are willing to sacrifice on behalf of the community."

Encouraging young people who are international in their experience and outlook to involve themselves in politics and government also has other benefits. Oyun-Erdene believes it can help to root out persistent systemic flaws that are holding the country back: corruption and nepotism.

The fight against corruption

Raila Odinga, an opposition politician in Kenya, said in a campaign speech in 2022 that his country has four enemies: poverty, ignorance, disease, and corruption. All these problems would be solved, he said, "if we eliminate the last enemy, corruption." He added: "Without ending corruption, we cannot prosper, enlighten or heal our people." Oyun-Erdene nods in agreement when I mention this statement.

Like many developing economies, Mongolia has long been plagued by systemic corruption—and people are sick and tired of it. It has caused critical projects, including key railway lines and renewable energy schemes, to stall or even fail. It's a reason for continuing environmental damage in the mining industry and for illegal trade with neighboring countries that undermines the Mongolian economy. It delays, distorts, and diverts economic growth.

Corruption both causes and thrives upon weaknesses in economic, political, and social institutions.

Again, corruption is not unique to Mongolia. There will always be room for greedy people whose aim is to take advantage of the system to fill their own coffers at the cost of the general population. The corridors of power are dimly lit in many countries, and even in the most robust democracies, individuals are fallible and institutions vulnerable. In a sense, the fleas come with the dog. But there are also some aspects of Mongolia that make it especially vulnerable. One is its geographical location: Mongolia comes under constant pressure from its authoritarian neighbors and main trading partners, Russia and China, with businesspeople and politicians from these countries ever alert to opportunities for meddling in Mongolian affairs, according to several interviews and reports. Another aspect is poverty. The links between corruption and poverty run in both directions: corruption deepens poverty, but poverty also invites corruption. Perhaps the main factor driving graft in Mongolia, however, is its economic dependency on one of the world's shadiest industries: mining. According to the corruption watchdog Transparency International, the sector is uniquely exposed to corruption risks due to its technical complexity, the involvement of large sums of money, and the blurred lines between private and public sector interests. Moreover, corruption risks exist at every stage of the value chain, from the awarding of contracts and licenses to the regulation and monitoring of operations, the collection of taxes and royalties, revenue distribution and management, and the implementation of sustainable development policies and projects. Given the mining sector's outsized role in the Mongolian economy, it seems especially vital that it should be characterized by transparency, accountability, and an absence of corruption. The reality, however, is often quite the opposite.

In December 2022, while I was researching and writing this book, the biggest corruption scandal in Mongolia's modern history hit the headlines. It was covered by most major international news organizations, including Bloomberg, the *Financial Times*, and the *Economist*, as well as all the larger Asian outlets. It's not often that corruption cases in smaller countries far away from Wall Street or the City of London grab that amount of attention. But this case—whose protagonists were labeled "The Coal Mafia"—had all the elements of a juicy thriller. There were even rumors about a plot to assassinate the prime minister.

"Yes, I've heard about this," Khishgeegiin Nyambaatar, minister of justice, tells me in an interview. "I myself have felt threatened and I've been worried about my own safety. The prime minister is in good hands with his security detail. We are in the process of breaking systemic corruption. This will anger many people. But that does not stop us. We cannot be afraid; we must reach our goal."

During a brunch interview at the prime minister's residence, a modernistic building located in a closed-off valley south of the city, I ask him how he has coped with such threats. He says that he and his wife have had long discussions about the situation and that security has been increased.

On his desk is a biography of Shinzo Abe, the former prime minister of Japan who was shot and killed at a political campaign event in July 2022. Oyun-Erdene attended the funeral in Tokyo (just a week after attending Queen Elizabeth II's in London) and it's evident that it had an emotional impact on him that has resonated all the more in light of intelligence reports at home.

"It's very sad, but political leaders who are making reforms . . . it's not very easy," he says with a tense smile. "After the funeral I shared my feelings with my wife and said that [Shinzo Abe] did a lot of good for his country. The ending of a public servant can be good or bad, and some leaders who make large reforms sometimes have sad endings. You have to be ready for risks. The responsibility has been assigned to me as the country's leader. This corruption must stop."

Hearing his three-year-old daughter (the youngest of three children) playing and laughing with a friend right outside the room we're in, a reminder that threats have an impact on a leader's entire family, doesn't make the conversation easier.

But back to the Coal Mafia. Thousands of Mongolians took to the streets—yes, in Sükhbaatar Square—after it was revealed that a network of business executives and high-ranking politicians had been stealing coal from a state-owned mining company and selling it across the border in China. An investigation showed that huge amounts of coal revenues had been embezzled into private accounts rather than placed in government coffers. The scheme had been running for years. Crowds of mostly youngish Mongolians flocked to the square in temperatures well below freezing to show their disgust. After an initial attempt to storm the main government building, the protests were mostly peaceful. The scene recalled the demonstrations in the same square three decades earlier that toppled Mongolia's erstwhile communist regime.

"People who steal public funds should be held accountable just as someone who commits a crime is held responsible," a 24-year-old woman at the scene, named Bolormaa Bayarmagnai, told Reuters. "We would like to use that money efficiently for development in our country."

The protesters demanded accountability from the government on the issue at a time when funds were desperately needed to help the country negotiate economic hardships brought about by a global economic downturn in the wake of the pandemic. In a significant development, however, the grievances being aired began to extend beyond the coal heist. As the protests continued over several weeks, more and more people showed up in support, bringing their own issues and complaints with them: air pollution, the lack of job opportunities, inequality in society, and various other issues that can be traced to corruption. As mentioned, the incident also fueled bitterness that had already found an outlet in earlier protests expressing generalized dissatisfaction ("Do your job!") with the government.

As he had done during those earlier demonstrations, Oyun-Erdene went—against the advice of his security team—to meet with protesters outside on the square, to try to explain to them how his government was working to crack down on corruption, improve the economy, and fight social inequality. The prime minister tells me he was also concerned about preventing any clashes between protestors and the police, as the memory of five people dying during similar protests in 2008 remains an open wound. And besides, he wanted to "join forces" with the protesters in their opposition to corruption. Predictably, he struggled to make himself heard over their chants.

The coal theft was discovered by the government after it compared Mongolian export data with import data reported by China. During an investigation, it was revealed that significant amounts of coal had been exported to China without any Mongolian customs registration. Inspectors determined that thousands of truckloads of coal had instead been registered as "empty" at customs.

The state-run mining company Erdenes-Tavantolgoi JSC holds licenses for the Tavan Tolgoi coal deposit in the southern Gobi Desert, one of the largest deposits of high-quality coking and thermal coal in the world. The coal is dug up and trundled in fleets of trucks—and increasingly by a new railway—across the desert to China. This operation is managed by Erdenes Tavan Tolgoi (ETT), another state-owned entity with a far from pristine reputation: "It has long been a byword in Mongolia for callousness and mismanagement," the *Economist* wrote in a report on the scandal. The coal from Tavan Tolgoi is highly prized in China, where it is used in the production of steel. In all, a staggering 385,000 tons of it is known to have gone missing over the years, but the true figure is possibly much more. Some say the amounts reported are just the tip of the iceberg.

It didn't take long for the handcuffs to come out, and it's not hard to imagine how panic must have taken hold among those directly or indirectly involved. The rumors of a plot to assassinate the prime minister conceivably stem from desperate attempts to stop the investigation. Several executives of the state-run companies, as well as members of their families, were arrested, as were numerous parliamentarians and other high-ranking politicians. Mongolia's anti-corruption body even confirmed that a former president, Khaltmaagiin Battulga, was among those being investigated.

"Even if I lose my position, the investigation against the systemic corruption, against the Coal Mafia, will not be stopped," Oyun-Erdene says. "This is just the beginning. The good thing is that many young people and young leaders now have understood the 'black market' system. The truth has been revealed."

At time of writing, more than 140 people are under prosecution, according to Khishgeegiin Nyambaatar. But many more heads might roll as the investigation widens—perhaps enveloping the uppermost tiers of the administration. Some politicians might find themselves being probed not for having benefited from the scam directly but for having covered for people who did. A spokesperson for China's Foreign Ministry has said Beijing stands ready to assist investigators if required.

Gantumur Luvsannyam, of the Democratic Party, acknowledges the importance of fighting corruption, but he believes the government's approach is lacking in one fundamental respect: it doesn't tackle the root cause of the problem. The most important ingredient to root out corruption, he says, is to introduce economic liberalization and create a business environment where people can make good money the legal way—without feeling the urge to bend the rules.

"Fighting corruption is a good thing," he tells me. "But we must strive to create an environment where it's non-existent. We need to change the management system, the way we do business. If the system is not changed, and they remove all the corrupt people, the system is going to create new corrupt people."

He adds: "Now, it's just a change of guard. Some people will go to jail for whatever crimes they did, and the next day new people will come in and commit the same crime."

It's difficult to calculate precisely how much money was stolen or went missing, but estimates range from hundreds of millions to billions of US dollars. Many of the transactions appear to have been made as payments in kind, where goods or services are offered instead of cash. Some deals were deliberately underpriced, some overpriced. But perhaps the biggest cost, according to Khishgeegiin Nyambaatar, is in lost opportunities—state funds having been deprived of financial resources that could have been used to improve infrastructure or build a better society.

Over the last three decades, Mongolia's GDP per capita has increased more than tenfold, but poverty levels have hardly moved:

around a third of the country remains grounded in poverty. Khish-geegiin Nyambaatar puts the blame firmly on graft.

"During these years we have expanded the economy but not human development," he tells me. "The main reason, we think, is systemic corruption associated with state-owned companies."

The state-owned Development Bank of Mongolia (DBM), established a decade ago to finance important projects, has also been subject to public anger over corruption allegations. The government launched a probe into the bank a few years ago, and its criminal investigation has targeted a dozen debtors—including high-profile lawmakers.

Like Oyun-Erdene, Khishgeegiin Nyambaatar spent his youth in the mining town of Berkh, and he explains that the two have been talking about how to root out corruption ever since entering parliament together in 2016. Their shared working-class background, he adds, has given them a common set of values.

"We want to clean the system of corruption and leave a healthier society to our children," the justice minister says.

Although Mongolia has ratified the United Nations Convention against Corruption and tough anti-corruption measures are being taken, people here talk of graft schemes large and small being part of everyday reality. In a 2021 poll conducted by the IRI, 65 percent of respondents named corruption as one of the top issues facing Mongolia. Several international reports also highlight its graft culture as a significant impediment to investment. All of which makes the government's anti-corruption push an essential part of its mission to modernize Mongolia.

The current administration has passed several laws, and at the time of writing had further bills pending, aimed at creating greater transparency in government. Oyun-Erdene's administration has even declared 2023 an "anti-corruption year" and has been carrying out a five-part plan based on advice from Transparency International. The legal framework for doing business in Mongolia, Khishgeegiin Nyambaatar insists, must be made clearer, so that local and international investors can feel their investments in the country are safe and viable.

While the Coal Mafia scandal was a great embarrassment to the nation and its mining sector, it also offered a golden opportunity for anti-corruption forces to take action. As the saying goes, "Never let a serious crisis go to waste." In other words, take the opportunity to do things you couldn't do before. In the scandal's wake, several government figures tell me, solutions have been put in motion to end years of shady business deals.

"I like the protesters," Nagi Otgonshar, vice minister at the Ministry of Mining and Heavy Industry at the time of our interview, tells me. "They opened an opportunity for us to push through reforms quicker. We could really take advantage of the situation."

The reforms he's referring to entail a massive dose of transparency being introduced into the mining sector and Mongolian business more generally. Starting in early 2023, Erdenes-Tavantolgoi JSC ceased signing direct sales contracts with buyers in China. Instead, the company's coal is auctioned on the Mongolian Stock Exchange. Authorities argue that selling coal through the stock exchange will prevent theft and backroom deals, that it will improve transparency, and ultimately net higher returns for the state. In the past, by contrast, state-owned companies signed purchase and sales agreements with buyers they favored, and they did it behind closed doors. Under the new system, any buyer will be able to open an account and participate in coal purchasing through licensed brokers on an equal playing field. It's a big step.

On the horizon, the government also plans to widen the auction system to other minerals. Potential commodities to be traded include copper, iron ore, gold, fluorspar, and molybdenum. Commodity exchanges can be useful in bringing together buyers and sellers in markets with relatively low trading volumes, as they reduce counterparty risk, because the exchange acts as the counterparty for both buyer and seller in each deal. Trade on the exchange will remain limited in volume until it can replace the long-term contracts preferred by Chinese buyers. The country expects to sell 50 to 60 percent of its annual coal exports through the exchange in 2024 and to fully switch to online trading by 2025.

Zolbayar Enkhbaatar, editor-in-chief at *Inside Mongolia*, a market intelligence newsletter, believes the commodities market can help the government win back some of the trust lost during the coal-thieving fiasco. "Mongolians seem to regard the stock exchange as a symbol of transparency," he told Al Jazeera in January 2023. "The coal theft was possible because the involved companies lacked transparency: no one could see how they were selling coal and to whom they were selling it."

Another move to increase transparency was in fact instigated months before the Coal Mafia saga came to light, when the Mongolian Parliament approved plans to transfer several state-owned companies to partial public control by floating them on the stock exchange. (This follows the theory that publicly listed companies typically have higher transparency than do private companies, as they are required to disclose their financial statements, annual reports, and other relevant information to the public and regulators. State-controlled enterprises, by contrast, notoriously lack transparency.) Mongolia Telecom Company, Information Communication Network, Information Technology Park, and various road maintenance companies were included in this reform, up to 34 percent of the firms being transferred to public control via brokers.

"The decision to open up these state-owned assets and place them in public control [via the stock market] is a vital step in making them fit for the future and in driving the wider modernization of the Mongolian economy," Deputy Prime Minister Amarsaikhan Sain-buyan commented at the time.

Following the coal scandal, a third of the shares in ETT are also being sold on the stock exchange, again with transparency front of mind. In addition, the government promised to make whole-sale reforms to the management of Erdenes-Tavantolgoi JSC, hire employees in a transparent process, and eventually make it a public company.

Furthermore, the country's most systemically important banks—The State Bank, XacBank, Khan Bank, Trade & Development Bank, and Golomt Bank—were all recently required to float shares on the stock exchange, in a move designed to increase transparency in the financial markets. Fitch Ratings wrote in a comment that the push for Mongolia's banks to be listed, and to cap any single stake at 20 percent, will "improve transparency and strengthen the banking sys-tem's corporate governance," ultimately enhancing its stability. "We expect a listed bank to provide more timely and detailed disclosure, not only in its financials but also its banking operations, allowing more public participants' oversight," the agency said at the time.

Meanwhile, corruption's next door neighbor, political nepotism, has been another constant in Mongolian public life.

Ask people here how they feel about politicians, and you'll get an earful. The resentment runs deep in relation to perceived favoritism and sleaze. If a new minister or official is appointed, it's far from unheard of that he or she will fill key positions with close friends over better-qualified candidates. But it gets even worse than that: in 2018, it was reported that political positions in Mongolia had in fact been up for grabs by those willing to pay. Both of the major political parties, the Mongolian People's Party and the Democratic Party, were the targets of protests that year after allegations surfaced of a "pay to play" scheme in which high-level government positions were essentially being sold. It's not hard to imagine what kind of politics and society you end up with when high-ranking government positions are available to the highest bidder, and neither good governance nor fairness and equality are what springs to mind.

Prime Minister Oyun-Erdene, who normally speaks in very calm tones, has trouble hiding his frustration when talking about government officials and parliamentarians who abuse the system for personal gain. "Some leaders are drawn to corruption, and they become corrupt because they're not able to control their hunger for power and greed," he says.

He continues by expressing his distaste for populism and "parliamentarians who don't represent the people," two things that he says undercut economic progress and trust in democratic institutions. "If we have political instability, we will have economic instability and it will lead to social crisis. In order to have the middle class as a majority of our society, we need reforms, including reforms of the government, reforms for the social welfare system, reforms of the economy."

Measuring any tangible progress toward rooting out corruption and nepotism is no simple task. In 2022, Mongolia ranked 116th, six places lower than in 2021, in Transparency International's "corruption perceptions index," based on surveys of businesspeople and experts. However, Khishgeegiin Nyambaatar believes this apparent decline can be explained by the fact that the country had just done the hard work of exposing various examples of large-scale corruption. As it continues to fight such corruption, he insists, its ranking will improve.

For its part, the Financial Action Task Force, a global watchdog, has removed Mongolia from its dreaded "gray list" of countries with flawed systems and says the country has made "progress in strengthening measures to tackle money laundering and terrorist financing." And the World Bank contends that, through its adherence to democratic principles and its pursuit of transparency, Mongolia has "the chance to break out of this cycle [of political corruption]."

It's not hard to understand why people are still skeptical about the government's drive. They have, of course, heard similar promises before. An American-Mongolian woman in her late 20s tells me that "all politicians say they are fighting corruption, but they are all equally corrupt themselves."

Erik Versavel, a Belgian banker, writes in his book *Mongolia: Cracks in the Eternal Blue Sky*, that "the country will remain an economic and financial shadow of what it potentially could be" over the coming years because of political instability. But, on a note of buoyancy, he adds: "As we have gotten to know the Mongolian people, and their skills, optimism and capabilities, we must hope and believe that one day an inclusive society with opportunities for all comes to exist and flourish."

Time will tell if the administration's anti-corruption push leads to long-lasting systemic change—or if the fleas just keep clinging to the dog.

"Switzerland of Asia" vs "Mongolian barbecue"

On a frosty January day, I unexpectedly found myself in a room full of people in colorful costumes and oversized hats. It was World Religion Day, and the occasion was being celebrated in a hotel function hall in central Ulaanbaatar. All of the leading faiths were represented, including the three Abrahamic religions, Buddhism and Hinduism, and lesser-known religions such as Zoroastrianism, Babism and the Baháʼí Faith. There were also representatives of non-religious, humanist groups, as well as people from the UN, the US embassy, and other sections of the diplomatic community.

What was striking about the event was not so much the varied customs on show but for me an unexpected sense of unity and harmony between the different religious leaders. It's easy to imagine how a gathering between such diverse faiths might end up in bickering over points of theology, who will be welcomed into God's kingdom, who the infidels are, and so on. But here, the atmosphere was quite the opposite. The clerics offered blessings to each other. A Jewish rabbi read in Hebrew from the Torah, a group of Buddhists chanted meditative verses, a Japanese Shinto priest offered his blessings to all present, and so on. I've never seen anything like it.

The aim of World Religion Day, a global celebration with a long tradition of observance in Mongolia, is to promote understanding and peace among all religions. And the theme this time was social equality, giving leaders the chance to speak more about "real-world" themes than spiritual ones.

"Father, we are grateful for the freedom of religion here in Mongolia," said a Christian priest. "As we are experiencing social and economic challenges, please . . . give peace and hope to every heart in Mongolia."

The Hindu representative, meanwhile, said that where inequality exists between different peoples, there can never be social progress.

But perhaps the most striking comment came from the adherent to Bahá'ísm, a movement started in the 19th century that extols the essential worth of all religions and the unity of all people: "A financier with colossal wealth should not exist while near him is a poor man in dire necessity. When we see poverty allowed to reach a condition of starvation it is a sure sign that somewhere we shall find tyranny."

Convergence of views and the sowing of peace and social harmony among diverse—or even at times purportedly irreconcilable—groups are perhaps not as unusual as it may seem, however. Not in Mongolia, at any rate. The country in fact has a long—and to many in the West, unknown—history of hosting regional and international peace talks. Sometimes referred to as "the Switzerland of Asia" for its open foreign policy and neutral status, the nomad nation plays an important role in ensuring peace and security in the region, according to several international observers.

"Despite being landlocked, Mongolia's creative foreign policy, that prioritizes dialogue and co-operation, serves as a bridge between countries," UN Secretary-General António Guterres said in Ulaanbaatar in August 2022.

During his visit, Guterres applauded Mongolia for its commitment to non-proliferation and disarmament by declaring itself a nuclear weapon-free zone, saying that he hopes other countries might follow Mongolia's example "so we can realize a world free of nuclear weapons." The secretary-general's visit also coincided with the 20th anniversary of Mongolia's participation in UN peacekeeping operations. In fact, Mongolia is the country that allocates the highest per capita contribution to peacekeeping in the world.

Regarding Mongolia's role as a regional peace mediator, Guterres referred specifically to the Ulaanbaatar Dialogue Initiative on North-East Asian Security, a unique forum for multilateral talks. Since its establishment in 2014, it has served as a non-traditional mediation platform where representatives from Northeast Asian countries can discuss security issues impacting the region. Initially inspired by the Helsinki Accords of 1975, a watershed moment of détente in the Cold War, its aim, according to Mongolia's Ministry of Foreign Affairs, is to help defuse tensions on the Korean Peninsula and promote confidence building and peacemaking. Within the context of the rise of China (and its escalating diplomatic feud with the US) and of Russia's belligerence in Europe, Mongolia has come to occupy an increasingly pivotal position on the geopolitical map. As alliances take shape on both sides of the Ukraine war, the Ulaanbaatar Dialogue may yet serve as a conspicuously vital platform.

Mongolia abstained on the UN General Assembly vote condemning Russia but has sent emergency humanitarian assistance to Ukraine. In Ulaanbaatar, the Russian invasion was denounced by the main opposition Democratic Party, whose representatives tell me they are disappointed that the government hasn't pushed harder to support Kyiv. Instead, the government has pleaded for international understanding of its precarious position as a democracy squeezed between two authoritarian neighbors, both of them seemingly on an increasingly militarized collision course with the West. Mongolia indeed walks a tightrope on Ukraine.

Meanwhile, the country continues to help maintain a finely poised balance on the Korean Peninsula. Diplomats from Japan and North Korea—two countries that don't share official diplomatic relations—met for discussions in Mongolia in 2019, and (as mentioned), the country was considered as a host for the 2018 talks between former US President Donald Trump and North Korea's leader, Kim Jong Un, due to having good diplomatic relations with both nations. (Ultimately the meeting was held in Singapore, some insiders indicating the real reason for the Southeast Asian city-state's selection was Trump's desire to take Kim out for a round on one of its famed golf courses.)

Mongolia's role as a force for diplomatic stability in the region is not a recent phenomenon. The phrase *Pax Mongolica*, Latin for "Mongol peace," describes a period of relative stability in Eurasia for the conquered peoples of the Mongol empire and along the trade routes of the Silk Road during the 13th and 14th centuries. It was commonly said that "a maiden bearing a nugget of gold on her head could wander safely throughout the realm." What's more, Chinggis Khan is also responsible for establishing the framework of diplomatic immunity for ambassadors and diplomats, setting a new benchmark for international relations.

"Usually how they declared war on one another's nations was to kill the ambassador—that was the beginning of it," Jack Weatherford, the author of *Chinggis Khan and the Making of the Modern World*, has been quoted as saying. "But Chinggis Khan said 'no, every ambassador must be protected with your life.' So, he created the station of diplomatic immunity. He created international trade and international law and to me these are two of the greatest achievements of Chinggis Khan."

In other words, the Mongols sought not merely to conquer the world but to institute a global order based on free trade and the rule of law. One might say that the defense of such cornerstones is increasingly vital in today's world, as trade wars, decoupling, and disintegration look to be in the process of replacing decades of globalization based on rules and cooperation. (You can read more about how to navigate this new world of trade conflicts and decoupling in my 2020 book, *The Epic Split*.)

Mongolia's gift for diplomatic arbitration is still very much apparent today and is manifested in its so-called "third neighbor" foreign policy. While Mongolia shares hard borders with its two giant neighbors, Russia and China, the idea of a third neighbor refers to other countries that Mongolia has built relationships with, as a way to balance the influence of the northern bear and southern dragon. The term was reportedly first used by US Secretary of State James Baker, in reference to his own country, during a meeting during a visit to Mongolia in 1990. The policy has since received much attention from international scholars and is generally hailed as an effective way of building goodwill and unity on democratic principles.

"Mongolia has no alternative but to keep healthy relations with its neighbors, but that fact does not negate Ulaanbaatar's commitment to democracy or its 'third neighbor' policy," writes Bolor Lkhaajav, a Mongolian scholar, in an article for the Japanese website The Diplomat. "While relations with China and Russia [have] irreplaceable value for Mongolia's economy, what is equally important to Mongolia is each state's peaceful, non-threatening existence and multilateral collaborations."

Foreign commentators, meanwhile, can almost be said to have lined up to praise Mongolia for its commitment to democracy. In a speech in December 2022, US Ambassador to Mongolia Richard Buangan said that America's relationship with the country is important for reasons of shared ideals. "Most importantly, Americans and Mongolians share the same values: a belief in democracy, human rights, free and fair private sector growth, and the sovereignty of nations," he declared. "We appreciate Mongolia's role as a model of democracy in this region. The United States is committed to partnering with Mongolia as it strengthens its democratic institutions and diversifies its economy. Mongolia, in turn, has reinforced democracy throughout the world, its hosting of a Community of Democracies conference in 2013 as one prominent example."

The Community of Democracies is a global intergovernmental coalition of member states that support common democratic values and standards. The US ambassador also commended Mongolia's improved bilateral business environment and the way economic cooperation and mutual prosperity had underpinned the two countries' 35 years of diplomatic ties.

"Part of that cooperation has involved working together to strengthen Mongolia's free-market economy and tackle investment climate challenges," he added. "Overcoming those challenges will create the conditions to attract more investors. The business community has praised Mongolia's commitment to improve current legislation, and we too applaud this commitment. An effective, transparent legislative process, much like the one offered by our bilateral transparency agreement, would engage affected parties as legislation is being deliberated to ensure the business community's input is considered.

"Fair and predictable legal systems will go a long way towards attracting and sustaining businesses, allowing them to thrive and providing prosperity to Mongolia's people. This is a matter of political will—the will to make tough decisions; to guide legislation transparently; to implement laws fairly; and to hold all parties to [account]."

Buangan also highlighted military cooperation, a touchy topic as geopolitical tensions have escalated dramatically in recent times between the US and both of Mongolia's neighbors. "We appreciate the strong ties our two militaries have developed and congratulate Mongolia on 20 years of UN peacekeeping operations," the ambassador said. "The US military has worked closely with the Mongolian armed forces to provide training, equipment, and facilities to support Mongolian troops on UN peacekeeping missions."

As the scope of Mongolia's third neighbor policy has evolved, it has also faced challenges. The term was frequently used by American leaders such as George W. Bush in recognition of Mongolia's liberal democratic reforms and its efforts to join the so-called coalition against terrorism. However, this caused a perception that Mongolia sought to promote a US agenda, causing some mistrust from Russia and China.

Daniel Kawczynski, a British Member of Parliament who is also a trade envoy to Mongolia, tells me that helping Mongolia limit its vulnerability to overdependence on either China or Russia is of strategic importance to Britain, adding that London sees Mongolia and other friendly Asian nations as increasingly important markets for British businesses.

I first ran into Kawczynski at a Chinese restaurant in the Shangri-La complex in Ulaanbaatar as he was visiting with a trade delegation of British companies, and we arranged to speak online when he returned home to his constituency in Shrewsbury, an English market town.

"Mongolia is a breathtakingly beautiful country with extraordinary traditions and culture," he tells me in our interview. "I liked the Mongolian people instinctively. I'm very appreciative of their culture and their enthusiasm to want to engage with us. We see Mongolia as a very important beacon of democracy in the whole region."

Born in Warsaw, Poland, under Soviet rule, Kawczynski doesn't have a great many positive things to say about authoritarian regimes and their human rights violations. To illustrate Mongolia's vulnerability, he tells me a story from when he was a child and went to the zoo in Warsaw.

"There, in a tank, I saw a snake that was sleeping. And in the corner of the tank was a little mouse—it had been put in the tank by the zoo staff. The mouse was awake, and it could see that the snake was asleep. The mouse knew that when the snake wakes up, that is the end. We've seen what Russia and China are capable of. So, the Mongolians in their determination to maintain their democracy are very brave people, and people that we want to support."

But even as the country is applauded by diplomats, trade envoys and development bankers, and by the many outsiders who do business here, or who visit for adventures in Mongolia's wild countryside, few people around the world are remotely aware of the nation's actual capabilities, or its potential.

In fact, when I speak with people from different parts of the world, some—actually quite a few—conflate Mongolia with Inner Mongolia and assume it to be part of China. (Inner Mongolia was part of the Mongolian empire at its height but did not cede with modern-day Mongolia when the latter gained independence from China in 1911.) Others even think that Mongolia is simply an ancient empire lost in history, much like Mesopotamia or the Ottoman empire. Several Mongolians interviewed for this book express frustration at having to repeatedly explain, when they're abroad, what Mongolia actually is—and how democratically and technologically advanced it is. Grace Jacobsen, a blogger previously based in Mongolia, wrote in a tongue-in-cheek post titled "10 facts people should know about Mongolia" that many foreigners aren't aware Mongolia is in Asia and not Africa (they get confused with Angola), that people here speak Mongolian, not Chinese, and that they eat mutton and not "BD's Mongolian Grill."

Prime Minister Oyun-Erdene cites the concept of Mongolian barbecue—now served in restaurants all over the world—as an example of the lack of knowledge about his country and its culture. Although Mongolians have some of the best meat on the planet and are masters at firing up a tasty grill, there's nothing officially called "Mongolian barbecue" here. It's purely a foreign invention, similar to how in China you won't find fortune cookies even though they're popular in Chinese restaurants in the US. In fact, the international version of Mongolian barbecue isn't even strictly barbecue but rather a combination of Chinese stir-frying and Japanese teppanyaki.

Mongolian barbecue was initially created by the Chinese comedian Wu Zhaonan. A native of Beijing, Wu fled to Taiwan after the outbreak of the Civil War in China and opened a street food stall in Taipei in 1951. While he initially wished to name his food "Beijing barbecue," he eschewed that idea due to political sensitivities (Beijing had just been designated capital of the People's Republic of China) and instead settled on "Mongolian barbecue," notwithstanding the absence of any connection to Mongolia. Despite its relatively cheap and unsophisticated fare, Wu's food stall attracted a wide clientele, including diplomats and wealthy businesspeople, and numerous imitators sprang up around Taipei to capitalize on the food's popularity, all adopting names such as Genghis Khan, Great Khan, and Heavenly Khan. The concept later spread around the globe, eventually even to Mongolia, where the popular tourist joint BD's Mongolian Grill, in Ulaanbaatar, is actually part of an American franchise chain. In 2018, the *Taipei Times*, referring to Wu Zhaonan's style of cooking, wrote that "this Taiwanese dish has become popular throughout the world."

Innocent though it might seem, essentially this is a story about the misrepresentation of a country's culture and identity. "While fortune cookies have become a staple in Chinese restaurants, they have also become a fodder for ethnic stereotypes," states History. com, and the same could be said of Mongolian barbecue.

"I want people to understand Mongolia for its true identity," says Oyun-Erdene. "I don't want to be 'Mongolian barbecue.' I want true knowledge and understanding about Mongolia in the world. I also want Mongolian people to have true knowledge and understanding about Mongolia, about our identity."

Mongolian barbecue is perhaps less to worry about, however, when compared with another piece of "stolen" Mongolian cultural branding: the notorious Mongols Motorcycle Club. Originally formed in 1969, in Montebello, California, by mainly Hispanic members, the Mongols is considered one of the most dangerous and violent motorcycle gangs in America and has a long history of murder, assault, drug dealing, and robbery. Its insignia depicts a caricature of a Mongol warrior, and its first president reportedly named the club in honor of Chinggis Khan and the Mongol empire. Apart from that, there's no connection to Mongolia. In a discussion on the question-and-answer platform Quora, one user from Ulaanbaatar has branded the MC club a disgrace to the Mongolian people, and its members "fraudulent clowns."

Adding a twist to the matter of Mongolian barbecue is another example of what some might view as "cultural appropriation," and it's one that ties several themes of this chapter together. Often when popular foods come from one place but become associated with another, the new "host" country gains from the association. For example, the much-loved croissant has become an iconic symbol of France itself even though it actually originates from Vienna, Austria.

Swedish meatballs are supposedly from ancient Persia. For its part, Italy has certainly gained from its identification with ice cream, and you'd be forgiven for thinking Italians were indeed the inventors of this delicious, sweet treat. But you'd be wrong. The origins of ice cream—or so it's claimed—are in Mongolia.

According to the website A Foodie World, it all came about completely by accident. It's said that Mongolian horse riders would transport yak milk across the Gobi Desert in containers as a provision on long journeys, but when the temperature dropped, the milk, churning as they galloped, would freeze. As the Mongol empire expanded in the 1200s, so too did the popularity of this new iced-milk treat, and it's believed Marco Polo took the idea back to Italy at the end of the 13th century.

Perhaps confusion is the new normal in identity—no matter where you're from. Next to goals such as economic diversification and poverty reduction, finding a common identity—and shared national values—is a key pillar of the Mongolian government's vision to create a better and stronger society. Oyun-Erdene believes there's not only confusion internationally about Mongolia but among people on their own patch, too—partly due to the country having been "bombarded" with so many diverse and competing faiths, ideologies, and economic systems over the centuries, often with dramatic shifts from one century, or even generation, to the next. Mongolia has experienced feudalism, imperial rule, communism, liberalism, and capitalism. It has embraced democracy, having lived under authoritarianism. It has absorbed both Western and Eastern thought and ideologies. It has worshiped both Jesus and the Buddha. And its people, once conquerors of the world, have themselves been conquered.

"During the 13th century, Mongolians conquered and ruled the world," says Oyun-Erdene. "Then, under 70 years of socialism or communism, we lost our rights to speech, so we became 'speechless Mongolia'; we were controlled by others. Now, because of capitalism, many people worship Mr. Dollar."

He adds: "We cannot compete with other nations if we don't know who we are. If we have a common identity of the past, and of today, then this can create our identity of the future."

The government's goal under Vision 2050 is therefore "to create shared national values that can support the establishment of a nation deeply cognizant of the concept of national identity or distinctiveness by ingraining 'One Language, one history, one culture, and one belief.'" Even for a nation with a small population of 3.3 million people, however, agreeing on what constitutes a true national identity and national values will not come easy. In today's fast-paced, multicultural societies, discovering one's own personal, social identity, let alone feeling the way towards one shared with all of one's compatriots, is complex and challenging enough. That, at least, is something most of us can agree on.

So, what does it mean to be Mongolian? For a foreigner to understand and describe the identity of another culture, especially one as multilayered as Mongolia's, is perhaps a fool's errand, but most attempts shed at least some light.

The Swedish missionary and explorer August Larson, who lived on and off in Mongolia between 1893 and 1925, and who even became a duke in the country, wrote in his 1930 book, *Mongolia and My Life Among the Mongolians*, that: "The Mongols are a happy and cheerful people during peaceful times and level-headed and cold-blooded when there is danger on the way. They lead a healthy life; stay mostly outdoors and consume simple and healthy food. It is true that they are a very old race and have once conquered half the world, but they have never acquired or further developed any complicated outlook on life."

Put that in contrast with a more modern portrayal, from Lonely Planet's latest guidebook, of Mongolia's young tech-savvy and internationally minded city slickers: "Youth culture is highly influenced by Western TV, music, movies and social media. A thriving culture of rap music exists in Ulaanbaatar. You'll also spot skaters, Harley Davidson biker gangs, girl bands, punks and a handful of neo-Nazis. . . . In Ulaanbaatar many look like they've just stepped off the streets of New York or London, so convincing is their Western fashion sense. But talk to them and you'll soon realize that their hopes and dreams lie not only in the West but also in the future of Mongolia, its success, prosperity, and the continuation of its unique culture."

Almost a century apart, Larson and Lonely Planet offer very contrasting descriptions, but both contain truths about the country. It's a diverse culture, no question. If you come to Mongolia and want to learn about its identity, do visit the capital—but you should also travel to the countryside and the steppe. Stay with a nomad family and listen to the stories they tell; you'll learn both of the tranquility of being close to nature but also about the harsh realities of how life is lived far away from modern luxuries, especially in colder weather. When in Ulaanbaatar, visit the Narantuul Bazaar, the so-called black market. Strolling around its outdoor and indoor stalls affords as comprehensive a snapshot of Mongolia as you will find. Besides the usual cheap 'n' cheerful knock-off apparel and watches, you'll discover an exposition of just about everything that makes the world turn in Mongolia: saddles and other gear for horses and herding; handmade knives; leather boots and thick overcoats; musical instruments like the horse fiddle; non-electric sewing machines; solar panels; and of course distinctive Mongolian foods, notably *aaruul*, curdled yak or camel milk, and air-dried meats and cheeses. Even on a freezing day in January, the place buzzes, customers especially keen to take home thick carpets and garments of warm cashmere and yak wool.

A country's identity can, of course, also be found in its arts.

Zayasaikhan "Zaya" Sambuu is a world-renowned Mongolian painter. He grew up in a small town in the Gobi Desert during times of Soviet censorship, and he has always used his art to explore the way he feels about Mongolia, and about his Buddhist beliefs. After working internationally, exhibiting works in numerous different countries, and living as "a global nomad" for over a decade, he eventually settled back in Ulaanbaatar.

His studio, in a southern district of the city, is awash with his explosive and colorful works, which occupy easels, walls, tables, and every other available space the eye can see. Although being far from an expert on Mongolian art, I immediately recognize several of his paintings: I've seen them in designer stores and shopping malls across town.

"Those are copies and are sold everywhere; some might be genuine, but most are not," he tells me, seemingly unconcerned. As the saying goes, it's better to be copied than ignored.

He speaks—and paints—from both love and anger. In his work, Zaya promotes Mongolian culture, but he's also critical of it. When decision-makers and politicians try to hide parts of the country's history, by closing museums exhibiting sensitive topics, for example, Zaya takes that as his subject matter and splashes it on his canvases. "My message to such people is 'shame on you,'" he tells me, his eyes narrowing.

Zaya's work mainly consists of scenes of daily life in ancient times and exotic portraiture of nature, and he somehow connects the spirit of nomadic Mongolian art with Tibetan and Japanese traditional fine art techniques. Saatchi Art, one of the world's leading online art galleries, opines that Zaya bridges Mongolian traditional painting with contemporary international art, adding that he is "neither too conformist nor too modern."

One particularly striking painting depicts a young girl adorned with a set of pink headphones. There's something vulnerable about her, but she appears to be guarded by more ancient-looking female figures around her. From the perspective of an outsider to Mongolian culture, Zaya's works seem to offer up reflections on the country's past as well as its present.

Rock music fans, meanwhile, might have heard of The Hu, a sensational metal band that uses traditional Mongolian instrumentation. "Hunnu Rock," as the band has dubbed its sound, is a galloping, grooving kind of folk metal made with instruments such as the Mongolian guitar (*tovshuur*), the two-stringed horse head fiddle (*morin khuur*), the "jaw harp" (*tumur khuur*), and a three-fingered flute (*tsuur*), as well as throat singing.

"Our music is a blend of east and west, old and new," Galbadrakh Tsendbaatar, aka Gala, the band's lead singer, told the *Guardian* newspaper in 2019. "We're building on a history and a sound that has been around for thousands of years. That kind of knowledge must be passed on to the next generation—the history, the culture side has to be passed on—so it's really important to us."

One late night at a music club in Ulaanbaatar, I had the pleasure of drinking whiskey with some of the guys from The Hu, and they spoke passionately about traditional Mongolian music and of inspiring the next generation to uphold the cultural heritage it represents. Their first two videos, for the songs "Wolf Totem" and "Yuve Yuve Yu," have amassed more than 100 million views on YouTube, while their debut album, "The Gereg," opened at No 1 on Billboard's Top New Artist chart.

Meanwhile, a different kind of contemporary song—beautiful and melancholic—offers another glimpse of what it means to be Mongolian. "Tal Nutgiin Ohin" is by Ariu, a regular performer at the Fat Cat Jazz Club, possibly the best jazz joint in Asia. The YouTube video starts with her in downtown Ulaanbaatar, closed in by modern buildings, people pushing past her as cars honk on the roads. City life seems overwhelming; but in Ariu's mind, as the music plays in her earphones, she finds herself transported to the open steppe, wearing traditional clothes, and riding a horse as her hair blows in the wind—freedom all around. She sings: "Gazing at the horizon of the steppe. Caressing me, the tender wind." You won't get much closer to the Mongolian soul than that.

Such songs, by The Hu and Ariu, might signify that, in "the Switzerland of Asia," just as in the European Alps, or indeed America's prairie heartlands, the hills (and steppe) are alive with the sound of music. Perhaps Oyun-Erdene need only put on his earphones to find answers in his search for what unites the Mongolian nation.

2

Climbing mining's value chain

Mongolia's experience shows how subsoil riches can shape a whole society—and offers warnings about the need for diversification, balanced finances, and sustainability.

The sun is high in a cloudless sky, the air dry and dusty. From around a curve in the road, a yellow mining truck approaches with a roar, before slowing down and pulling in at a depot. The door swings open, and a woman in her late 20s, wearing round sunglasses and a hardhat, steps out onto a bridge-like contraption that helps her exit the vehicle for a shift change. The truck is as big as a villa, each tire taller than a person, and it has the capacity to carry over 300 tons of excavated soil.

We are at the Oyu Tolgoi (OT) copper mine in the southern Gobi Desert. The landscape feels naked and hostile. In front of us an open-pit mine gapes like a giant jaw, almost half a kilometer deep. It's as impressive as it is terrifying; one can imagine the massive wealth that's hiding under the surface and the hard work and engineering that goes into the whole enterprise, but at the same time it's hard not to be taken aback by the wounds that have been cut in the flesh of nature. Even the gigantic yellow trucks—colossal when you stand next to them—look like mere ants climbing up and down the edges of the abyss.

The young woman, named Dugaraa, explains that she has been driving these trucks for two years now and that it's a step up from her previous job in the catering industry, both in financial security and prestige. She's one of some 60 women who drive trucks and drillers at the site, making up a fifth of all vehicle operators.

"When I started, I was very excited but also nervous because the trucks are so big," she says. "My family were like, 'this is unbelievable.' Today, it's just part of my daily job. I'll keep doing it for as long as I'm healthy and happy."

She puts her sunglasses back on, nods farewell and swaggers off, looking healthy, happy, and full of confidence, like a character from a Luc Besson movie.

It is hard to exaggerate the importance of this mine, not just for people like Dugaraa but for Mongolia and its economic future. Located just 80 kilometers from the Chinese border, Oyu Tolgoi is one of the world's largest deposits of copper, a metal that's used in vast quantities both in renewable energy systems and for electric vehicles and that will therefore be vital as the world transitions away from carbon-intensive energy.

This region has a long history of using the metallic element. Bronze Age inhabitants once smelted it from an outcropping that the locals later named "Turquoise Hill"—Oyu Tolgoi—because the surface rocks were shot through with bluish copper traces. Now, after centuries of slumber, this mineral province has burst into life again, driven by demand associated with the dash for net-zero emissions.

Looking out over the endless moon-like landscape is nothing if not a dizzying experience. The entire site is bigger than Manhattan and will soon be deeper than the North Sea. It will account for some 5 percent of the country's economy as it reaches full capacity from 2023 onwards, simultaneously becoming the fourth-largest copper mine in the world. It is by far the biggest foreign-investment project in Mongolia and can be seen both as a bellwether for the country's overall openness to foreign financing and a blueprint for other megaprojects. It even has its own airport, and several flights transport commuters between Ulaanbaatar and the mine each day.

The on-site canteen that feeds the 6,000 miners is, unsurprisingly, the biggest in the country. At lunchtime, workers in orange, green, and other brightly colored overalls flood in like a tidal wave, filling the hall with chatter and laughter, then stream out just as seamlessly when the break is over. Such is its immensity that there's even a YouTube documentary about the canteen that has racked up millions of views. And the workers are not the only ones to sample the cuisine hereabouts; when we drove through the site, a handful of wild donkeys could be seen munching on the few straws of grass that grace an otherwise stony terrain.

Oyu Tolgoi is run by Rio Tinto, an Anglo-Australian multinational company that is the world's second-largest metals and mining business. Rio owns 66 percent of Oyu Tolgoi, the Mongolian state owning the remaining 34 percent. Deposits were first discovered in 2000 by Robert Friedland, a geologist and mining entrepreneur with a reputation for going where no one else dares in search of mineral riches. Resource-rich Mongolia is positioning itself as an alternative to China in the supply of minerals needed by the renewable energy and digitalization sectors, but it also recognizes that it needs help from foreign investors to develop the necessary mining infrastructure. Rio Tinto and Oyu Tolgoi offer the prime example of this.

The open-pit mine, it should be stated, is only the beginning of this colossal project: the real big bucks will come from underground mining. In January 2022, Rio's chief executive, Jakob Stausholm, and Prime Minister Oyun-Erdene Luvsannamsrai, together inaugurated the next part of the project by jointly pressing a button to detonate 6 tons of explosives. And so began the crucial work of underground caving.

Mining today remains as dangerous as it is loud. Ore at Oyu Tolgoi will be extracted from underground reserves through a method known as block caving. This involves undermining the solid ore mass—with explosions—to make it collapse under its own weight into a series of chambers from which the ore itself can be collected. The project involves creating 200 kilometers of tunnels at a depth of 1.3 kilometers. In many ways it represents the pinnacle of what modern mining engineers can achieve, and some of the world's most technically advanced and innovative suppliers of mining technology—including Denmark's FLSmidth and the Swedish-Swiss firm ABB—are onboard. I also meet a Mongolian man, the owner of a company that sells explosives and detonating systems, who tells me his firm was asked to supply products of a *higher* quality to the OT sites than elsewhere. (In hindsight, perhaps this ought to make one wonder a little about the safety levels at other Mongolian mining sites.)

"Even people who in general are against mining can't help but say 'Wooooooow!' when they visit the underground mine," one engineer tells me during my visit.

Safety instructions are to be found everywhere you look, for reasons that should be obvious enough. Everyone wears protective gear—hardhats, heavy boots, goggles, gloves, and yellow vests—and everywhere you go staff greet one another with "Have a safe day." On entering the site, everyone must submit to an alcohol test. (I passed. No, really!) I ask one of the engineers what kind of accidents one might expect if something goes wrong, and he paints a varied picture of sudden explosions, landslides, and leaks of contaminated water. Especially in the underground mine, explosions are the most feared hazard. There are even warning signs to drivers of smaller vehicles that they should beware of being crushed by the giant mining trucks. Duly noted.

The ore that is extracted from the mines is subsequently crushed into smaller and smaller parts. It's then taken on an overland conveyor from the primary crusher to a concentrator, which uses a series of mechanical and chemical processes to turn it into the final product, ready for export. This product is called concentrate, a fine powder that contains around 30 percent copper and smaller amounts of gold and other minerals. When holding it in the hand, it's as soft as flour and as black as soot but with small sparkles—like stars—of precious metal dust. It's then packed in big bags and shipped to China.

The roads connecting Oyo Tolgoi (and other Mongolian mining sites) to the Chinese border are often so busy that some truck drivers like to perform a tea ritual each morning that they believe helps them to stay safe on the road. The pearly *suutei tsai*—traditional milk tea with salt—is tossed into the sky as an offering to the spirits of the land, the deities of its shamanic ancestry.

And today it's not just the drivers who are praying for good fortune but the entire industry. Mining is the beating heart of the Mongolian economy, both directly and indirectly, and much of the country's financial and socioeconomic future lies in the aforementioned sooty concentrate. The sector accounts for almost 90 percent of the country's exports and more than 20 percent of all government revenues, according to data from the Mongolian National Statistical Office.

The vision of Mongolia's government—which in this chapter we will delve into some more—is essentially for the country's mining sector to ascend the value chain. In a nutshell, it wants to develop more lucrative and sustainable sites, in partnership with both local and international players, and to redistribute the revenues from such projects to the benefit of society as a whole and to support other sectors of the economy. It's a vision that's more easily declared than accomplished, but one that's nevertheless crucial to the country's overall progression.

Mineral miracle or resource curse?

Mining projects like Oyo Tolgoi don't come without controversies. Enormous reserves of gold and copper can bring prosperity to a country but with human, cultural, and environmental costs if not handled in a responsible and sustainable way. Resource-based economies have a long history of questionable outcomes for their people and for the cause of long-term political stability, and Mongolia has not been immune from such concerns.

Several reports over the years have highlighted the massive potential mining offers—and in the next breath warned about pitfalls such as corruption, the consequences of failing to reinvest revenues in people and infrastructure, and even political turmoil.

"Mongolia is on the verge of a mineral miracle," the *Harvard International Review* stated in a 2022 article. "It may not seem like it at first, but Mongolia could be a much wealthier nation within the next 20 years, on the level of the 'Asian Tigers' of the 1990s: Hong Kong, Singapore, South Korea, and Taiwan."

Mongolia has been called the "wolf economy," and for good reason: it's believed to be sitting on over $1 to 3 trillion worth of mineral resources, coal, copper, and gold making up the primary reserves. There are also deposits of rare earth metals, a key component in everything from mobile phones to missiles. For a country with a population of 3.3 million, that is enough to make everyone a near millionaire.

"On the other hand," the Harvard article continued, "Mongolia could remain in its current state, with its immense mineral resources bearing little fruit thanks to political inefficiency, economic downturn, and environmental destruction. What seems like a blessing could quickly turn into a curse, and Mongolia now finds itself at a fork in this road."

A curse, yes. This is a term that is often used when speaking to people about subsoil resources, not just in Mongolia but in general. The country has for years had its heels dug deep into mining dependency and today, according to several reports, it still risks succumbing to the "resource curse." Also known as "the paradox of plenty" or "the poverty paradox", this so-called curse is a well-observed phenomenon where countries with an abundance of natural resources—such as oil or diamonds—end up having *less* economic growth, *less* democracy, or *worse* development outcomes than countries with fewer natural resources have.

And then we have the Dutch Disease, a cousin to the resource course. This is another paradox, which occurs when good news—such as the discovery of large oil or mineral reserves—harms a country's broader economy. The term was coined to describe the decline of the manufacturing sector in the Netherlands after the discovery of a large natural gas field in the North Sea in 1959. The country's newfound wealth and massive exports of oil caused the value of the Dutch guilder to rise sharply, making exports of all non-oil products less competitive on the world market. Unemployment rose rapidly, and capital investment in the country dropped. Many other countries, such as the UK, Canada, and Russia, have all suffered from the disease to a greater or lesser extent.

Another effect of dependency on one single sector can be that it sucks up most of the local talent pool, stripping other sectors of skilled people. One example that comes to mind is Macau: even if a student graduates as an architect, dentist, or engineer, it's highly likely that he or she will end up dealing cards at a baccarat table, because the city's casinos dominate the economy.

Escaping these curses and diseases is not easy. Over 80 percent of the world's major oil and gas-producing economies and mining countries fail to meet "satisfactory standards" for managing their natural resources, according to a 2013 report by the New York-based Revenue Watch Institute, which tracks resource mismanagement and corruption. But there are also shining examples of how to manage a resource economy well, oil- and gas-rich Norway ranking as the top performer.

Mongolia's dependence on mining has in fact become harder and harder to ignore. Following the discovery of major coal deposits and gold-copper ore in the early 2000s, mining's economic significance quickly surpassed that of livestock, a traditional earner for the country, according to a report by East Asia Forum. Meanwhile, according to the Invest Mongolia Agency, more than 73 percent of all foreign direct investment (FDI) into the country between 1993 and 2017 was directed toward mining—from which evidence it should be obvious that Mongolia's economy is immensely vulnerable both to commodity-price and FDI shocks.

In 2022, mining accounted for more than a fifth of GDP, up from a tenth in 2000. During that period, however, the country's overall economic growth—which has skipped along at an average clip of 7.2 percent per year since the advent of large-scale mining in 2004, making Mongolia's one of the fastest-growing economies in the world—has obscured considerable macroeconomic volatility and frequent boom-and-bust cycles.

Mongolia's mining boom has in effect been a kind of roll-er-coaster expansion. A decade ago, Ulaanbaatar was on the frontier of global mining and had acquired the nickname "the Bangkok of the steppes" for its decadent and happy-go-lucky lifestyle. "Hotels are bursting; the Irish pubs, of which there are several, are heaving with foreign miners, investment bankers and young local women with very long legs and very short skirts," the *Economist* noted in 2012. The magazine, normally known for its cautious predictions, continued by saying that "Mongolia has a chance of becoming a Qatar or a Brunei: a country that has only a small population but almost all of it, in global terms, loaded," and that "Mongolia will be rich beyond the wildest dreams."

The country's upsurge was in reality the lucky—or perhaps unlucky—result of events far beyond its borders. In 2010, Austra-lia's coal mines suffered their worst floods in decades, halting coal exports to China. That prompted Chinese iron ore smelters to increase coal imports from their northern neighbor on a massive scale. In 2011, the Mongolian economy registered colossal growth of 17.3 percent, primarily due to a coal deposit at Tavan Tolgoi, located 240 kilometers from the Chinese border, and the copper deposit at Oyu Tolgoi. Share prices in mining companies active in the country surged, and in 2010 the Mongolian Stock Exchange recorded an increase of 121 percent, making it the world's best-performing stock market that year. The International Monetary Fund (IMF) expected growth to average 14 percent a year between 2012 and 2016. Mon-golia "is likely to grow faster than any other [nation] in the next decade," the *Economist* stated. Miners and investors were dancing to the beat of drillers and jack hammers like there was no tomorrow.

Then, the party ended. The mineral boom—which had earned the country the moniker "Minegolia"—turned out to be short-lived. The economic growth spurt came to a grinding halt in 2016, when mining prices fell and the economy of China, by far Mongolia's largest export partner, began to stagnate. The year before, in 2015, I had written a story for *Forbes* saying that China's declining appetite for energy, metals, and other commodities was bad news for several Asian commodity-producing countries—and predicted that Mongolia would take the worst beating. The national debt ballooned, and the country entered a period of economic crisis. By 2017, Mongolia was going cap in hand to the IMF for a $5.5 billion bailout. Today, the Mongolian people are neither loaded nor rich beyond their wildest dreams. Quite the opposite.

What happened to all the money made during the boom-and-bust years? That's a question many Mongolians are still asking. GDP per capita has been stuck at about $4,000 for the last decade, about the same level as Sri Lanka's, as mentioned. "Why are we still so poor when we have all these resources?" a woman in her mid-30s asked me, rhetorically, in a café in Ulaanbaatar, echoing the frustrations of an entire generation.

A 2020 report by the World Bank estimated that, out of every dollar in mineral revenues Mongolia has generated over the previous 20 years, only 1 percent was saved for future generations. That obviously points to a failure in governance. To make the situation worse, the country has not only consumed almost all of its mineral outputs, but it has also borrowed heavily against them, bequeathing negative wealth to the next generation.

"Instead of maximizing the benefits of its mineral wealth for diversified and inclusive growth, Mongolia has increasingly become more addicted to it," wrote Andrei Mikhnev, World Bank Country Manager for Mongolia, in the report. "At the same time, human capital has been underutilized and institutional capital has eroded."

He added: "Such inability to capitalize on the country's endowments has resulted in limited diversification of outputs and exports and has further amplified its vulnerability to the swings of the global commodity markets. Breaking this gridlock calls for a fundamental shift in approach that puts investing in minds on an equal footing with mines."

Economic growth had come almost entirely through capital accumulation and the intensive use of natural capital rather than through sustained productivity growth, the World Bank concluded. In other words, Mongolia had been dug up and sold to China.

(I can't help but think of the old saying among Wall Street investors, adapted from a Mark Twain quote: "A gold mine is a hole in the ground with a liar on top." While some of those standing atop the Mongolian mining industry have been well-meaning people, others seem to have been nothing but fools and liars.)

"It is an all-too-familiar story: A country strikes it rich, but the new avalanche of wealth poisons the political process, corrupts its institutions, distorts the economy and even creates pressures for secession," observed the Japanese magazine *Nikkei Asian Review* in an in-depth 2021 article on corruption in Mongolian mining.

After the mining boom came to an end a decade ago, share prices in mining companies active in Mongolia came tumbling down. At time of writing, the Mongolian Mining Corporation, the country's largest coal mining company, was still down 98 percent from its 2011 level on the Hong Kong stock exchange. Turquoise Hill Resources, the exploration firm which formerly operated the Oyu Tolgoi mine, dropped some 90 percent before being delisted as part of a buyout by Rio Tinto in 2022.

The lawsuits have flown, too. According to media reports, even Max Johnson, half-brother of former UK Prime Minister Boris Johnson, is in on the act, launching a $50 million lawsuit against Mongolia to try to recover an investment in a mining project that went horribly wrong. Mr. Johnson was in turn accused by a Mongolian businessman of making a false fraud complaint. The case is a mess, as are so many other similar disputes. Rio Tinto and the Mongolian government were at each other's throats for years before they managed to settle their feud. (More about that later in this chapter.)

The situation has in fact been so dire that one of the first things Oyun-Erdene did after becoming prime minister in 2021 was to officially apologize on behalf of the state for all the uncertainties about foreign investment since the 1990s. "On behalf of the Mongolian government, I apologize on all issues that have been unclear to investors for the past 30 years," he said. "As prime minister, I will do my best to revitalize the country's economy."

He added that "the Mongolian government will take responsibility if any foreign investment, agreements or megaprojects are stalled due to the fault of the Mongolian side." The government also announced the establishment of a new working group, chaired by Khishgeegiin Nyambaatar, minister of justice, to protect the interests of foreign investors.

But then the Coal Mafia scandal, as chronicled in Chapter 1, blew up in everyone's faces.

There is a long way to go to recuperate trust, but encouraging steps have been taken. Several observers say Mongolia stands on the cusp of a new mining boom—and that this time things are going to be different, social inclusiveness, sustainability, and long-term stability built in from the get-go. Various people within the government and mining sector tell me they have learned lessons from previous mistakes and that the country is ready to turn the page and write a new chapter.

Digging where you stand

Batnairamdal "Nagi" Otgonshar, at the time of our interview a vice minister at the Ministry of Mining and Heavy Industry, speaks with great intensity and passion—and leans so heavily on his elbows that I fear the table is going to tilt over.

"Yes! They—or we—should have done more ten years ago," he says. "But we also must acknowledge that it takes time to build capacity. Today, we have capacity. We have skill sets. We have national champions, whether they are state-owned, private, or public. We have international investors. Now, we'll take the next step. Mongolia's economy is at a leapfrog stage."

We meet at a swanky hotel bar named Wall Street, in downtown Ulaanbaatar. But even though we're light years away from the rough and tumble of the mining sites, giveaway signs are everywhere; for example, in the preponderance of men and women whose smart business suits are matched with dusty hiking boots.

Nagi is one of those Mongolians alluded to who studied at Harvard, embarked on a big-bucks international career, then decided to come back and support the country's development. Before becoming vice mining minister in 2020, he was already something of a known figure in certain circles thanks to a podcast he has been running for some years, called "Unlock." In each episode, he and a guest discuss a new non-fiction book, topics ranging from business management to philosophy or history.

One book that made an impression on him, and that connects to his work for the government and the ruling party, is *The World for Sale: Money, Power, and the Traders Who Barter the Earth's Resources*, by the journalists Javier Blas and Jack Farchy. It's a somewhat dystopian portrayal of the billionaire commodity traders who buy, hoard, and sell the earth's resources, and an eye-opening tour through some of the wildest frontiers of the global economy.

"From an economic perspective the book gives you the story of how commodity trading has become a huge part of the developing world," he says. "And we can actually link it to the 'coal theft' here in Mongolia. Where did the theft really come from? It came from the supply chain, from the trading. If we really are to take full advantage of our resources, max out potential revenue in every trade, then we really have to make the entire supply chain transparent—from trading to transportation."

Nagi was one of the main architects behind the government's Vision 2050 roadmap and worked as an advisor to the prime minister before joining the mining ministry. The mining sector is prioritized in the government's plan as a "keystone" in the development of sustainable economic growth that is beneficial to all, the wealth from mining to be distributed to support other sectors of the economy. The goal is to diversify and advance within the mining sector but also to diversify and advance the entire economy.

According to the roadmap, Mongolia will develop "responsible" mining and increase its processing capabilities before establishing "strategic and value-added mining megaprojects" and "evolving the mining sector as a responsible branch of the economy with minimum damage to nature." By adhering to strict international standards and norms, the government aims to put the wealth from mining deposits into economic circulation. Moreover, the country will "develop environmentally friendly and sustainable heavy industry with value-added cost production on the basis of processing mining raw materials and render support to advanced forms of investments."

Again, all of this will be easier said than done. However, if the country fails to lower its susceptibility to FDI shocks and global price fluctuations in raw materials, it risks being trapped in poverty. The opportunities as well as the challenges are great—and Nagi acknowledges both.

"We are still experiencing some symptoms of the resource course and it's a real threat," he says. "So is the Dutch Disease."

Reducing the risk of such curses, diseases, and paradoxes requires climbing the value chain in mining and boosting competitiveness in other sectors that stem from it. On the financial front, it is necessary to slow the appreciation of the real exchange rate as wealth racks up, while also harvesting profits carefully and saving them in special funds.

To capture profits for the benefit of future generations, and to fund strategic infrastructure projects, two separate national funds have been set up: a future heritage fund and a sovereign wealth fund. Among other things, these should help build Mongolia's resilience to external shocks and reduce its reliance on external borrowing.

The Future Heritage Fund, resembling Norway's Global Pension Fund, will accumulate mining revenues for the future and invest the proceeds exclusively outside Mongolia. The Ministry of Finance and the IMF project said that the fund should start accumulating around $125 million annually from 2023, coinciding with increased revenues from the Oyu Tolgoi copper and gold mine, according to a US embassy country report. Money accumulating in this fund can't be touched until 2030, and after that a maximum of 10 percent of net investable income can be spent each year.

The sovereign wealth fund's investments, meanwhile, will be domestically focused. Erdenes Mongol, a former state-owned enterprise that has been repurposed to manage the fund, is in practice a holding company for the country's state-owned mining companies. In many respects it's like a local version of Singapore's Temasek Holdings, one of Asia's most influential investment companies. Revenues from the companies under its umbrella can be moved into offshore investment accounts, where they can generate more cash. More critically, explains Nagi, the funds are thereby put beyond the grasp of politicians, who have a history of raiding government coffers ahead of elections to pay for populist projects.

To reiterate, then, one of these funds will be used to support future generations, while the other will be used for infrastructure and other large-scale projects that create jobs and build a stronger society. And the key to unlocking all of this will be for Mongolia to move up the value chain.

As the consultancy firm McKinsey noted in a 2020 report, mining's value chain—which encompasses everything from the extraction of raw materials to delivering products to customers— is the industry's backbone. Countries and companies that manage their value chains well can establish a significant source of competitive advantage and value creation. By contrast, those that neglect their value chains are likely to encounter bottlenecks and constraints that limit shipped throughput and yields.

Mining value chains currently face increased pressure from recent shifts in commodity markets—namely strong price fluctuations, shrinking value pools, changing market structures as new entrants make their presence felt, and tightened regulations—as well as from lingering uncertainties in the wake of the Covid-19 pandemic.

At the same time, environmental concerns continue to evolve, and new regulatory policies continue to be enacted. Companies face unprecedented pressures to increase their resilience, flexibility, and productivity, while also significantly reducing their environmental footprints to satisfy an intensifying push for disclosure by governments, investors, and stakeholders, according to McKinsey. Taking a closer look at the value chain from mine to market is therefore the first step in addressing these challenges.

And the best way to start, as the saying goes, is to dig where you stand.

"Mongolia is very much a mining-based economy, so the mining sector has the most competitive advantage in relation to any other industries in Mongolia," Nagi says. "Basically, every country invests heavily towards their most competitive industries."

He adds: "Mining, up to this point, has been very basic, with a very early stage of processing and then exports. So, mostly raw material exports. What we need to do now is move towards more processing and start moving onto the next level. This is our most competitive industry, so that's where the heavy infrastructure projects come in."

Nagi mentions a range of ongoing and planned projects aimed at reorienting the mining sector to value-added services as well as easier access to buyers. These include an oil refinery, a copper smelter, and a gold-washing plant, as well as better communications and energy infrastructure.

"We're talking about, like, billion-dollar projects," he says, adding that the country's ambition will open doors to bigger opportunities for both local and international suppliers and investors.

"There are many other potential large-scale mining projects, and if we build infrastructure these new mines would have relatively stronger competitive advantages. We have to ask ourselves, where do we want to see ourselves in 30 years?"

Of the planned megaprojects, the country's first oil refinery is among the grandest. It's being built in collaboration with the Indian civil engineering group Megha Engineering & Infrastructures, MEIL, and will be able to process 1.5 million tons a year, reducing Mongolia's dependence on Russia. The project is in fact a government-to-government deal involving India: it will be supported by a $1.24 billion soft credit line from New Delhi and has been hailed as a turning point in relations between the two countries. It will also make Mongolia self-sufficient in refined oil, and a net exporter. Today, Mongolia exports raw oil and imports back refined oil—far from an ideal business model. The goal is for the project to increase GDP by more than 10 percent, according to Nagi.

Another crucial mega project, although not directly linked to Mongolia's own subsoil riches, is Power of Siberia 2, a natural gas pipeline from Russia to China that travels over Mongolian land.

The venture is not without controversy. A joint statement released by Russia's President Vladmir Putin and China's Xi Jinping, in March 2023, reads: "The two sides will work together to promote studies and consultations on the new China-Mongolia-Russia natural gas pipeline project." But analysts warn the deal could further complicate an already adverse China-US relationship and raise geopolitical risks among major economies.

For Mongolia, the project would rake in cash by way of fees for allowing Russia and China to use its territory. What's more, Mongolia could also tap into the gas flow. By turning to gas, the country would cut its dependency on coal and thereby clean up its skies.

I ask the prime minister if he's not worried that Russia would always have the option to cut off that gas supply for political reasons, as Moscow did with its supplies to Europe over the Ukraine war. To stop supplying Mongolia, Oyun-Erdene replies, Russia would technically also have to cut its supply to China. "Can you imagine Russia shutting off the Chinese?" he asks rhetorically.

Nevertheless, it remains a controversial proposal, and feasibility studies and a public consultation are ongoing.

Another mega energy project that has raised a few eyebrows is the Erdeneburen hydroelectric power plant, financed by China. Although hydroelectric power is one of the oldest and largest sources of renewable energy globally, it doesn't come without baggage. Besides raising speculation about increased Mongolian reliance on China, there are environmental concerns: the project has the potential to damage the Ramsar wetlands in northwestern Mongolia. On the other hand, it would help to spur the transformation of Mongolia from an energy importer to an exporter.

Meanwhile, the inauguration in autumn 2022 of a new rail line connecting Mongolia's southern mining districts with the Chinese border is another boon for the country's miners. The Tavan Tolgoi railway has the capacity to export between 30 million and 50 million tons of coal to China annually, replacing transportation by trucks. "The launch of the rail service will no doubt greatly boost bilateral coal trade and lower costs," said Lin Boqiang, director of the China Center for Energy Economics Research at Xiamen University, as quoted by Chinese state media.

A green and elegant solution

Let's go back to the Oyo Tolgui site in the Gobi Desert. Business is running smoothly today, but relations between the Mongolian government and the Anglo-Australian mining giant were acutely sour for several years, mainly due to a combination of political turbulence and short-term thinking.

Mining can be a touchy topic. Over a number of years, local politicians have accused foreign mining investors of fleecing the country and damaging the environment. Sometimes these concerns have been genuine, sometimes populist fabrications or exaggerations to win popularity among voters. Even today, demonstrations in Ulaanbaatar by herders concerned about unregulated mining and water pollution are not rare. There are even YouTube videos showing baby camels born in the Gobi Desert with two heads or other deformations. I spoke on the phone with one local village leader who has been a vocal campaigner on the issue of deteriorating water quality—and whose finger has been clearly pointed at the nearby mines. What's certainly true is that such claims of environmental damage—well-founded or otherwise—and the ways they have been handled by the authorities, have sown friction and frustration.

Rio Tinto, for its part, has not enjoyed an untarnished reputation in a number of countries. As recounted by the *Economist*, it has stood accused at various junctures of destroying a historic site, poisoning rivers, and fostering a rotten workplace culture. These claims have forced the company to do some soul-searching, however, and to overhaul its management team.

Since then, Rio and Ulaanbaatar have managed to get their respective ducks in a row and reboot their relationship on a more collaborative footing. In January 2022, the two sides said they had reached an agreement to end their long-running dispute over financing and the expansion of the Oyu Tolgoi project.

"It's a major relief. It's a huge step forward for us," Rio's chief executive, Jakob Stausholm, told Reuters from Ulaanbaatar ahead of the ribbon-cutting ceremony alluded to, where he and Prime Minister Luvsannamsrai detonated several tons of explosives.

"We are very comfortable with this outcome and, more than anything, achieving a full reset of the relationship," said Stausholm, who became CEO in 2021, the same year that Oyun-Erdene took office in Mongolia.

As part of the agreement, Rio Tinto waived $2.4 billion in debt owed to it by the Mongolian government. This was a big deal. Indeed, according to several people I spoke to, it changes the entire financial outlook of the country.

Stausholm said the deal's multiple terms reflect "an elegant solution" to the complex issues that had previously strained relations with the government. "It is possible to do something for the benefit of the people of Mongolia and also for the benefit of our investors," he said. Oyun-Erdene, meanwhile, said the deal "demonstrates to the world that Mongolia can work together with investors in a sustainable manner and become a trusted partner."

Then, in March 2023, underground exploration at Oyu Tolgoi officially kicked off, Oyun-Erdene and Stausholm reconvening once again, this time 1,300 meters underground. They were both attired in orange overalls and hardhats with headlights—and wore beaming smiles on their faces.

"It's a great honor for me to speak to the world, from more than 1,000 meters underground, to state that Mongolia is on the way to becoming one of the foremost copper producers in the world,"

Oyun-Erdene said, unable to hide his emotion as he thanked staff and Rio Tinto for all their hard work over the years.

"Our journey wasn't easy, but we made it," he continued. "It shows the world that Mongolia is a trusted partner. Mongolia is open for all business. Mongolia is landlocked but not mind-locked. We have even more to offer in our non-mining sectors, including cashmere, tourism, energy, transportation, and logistics."

Inviting all present to share the "happy times of the Naadam holidays," in reference to the traditional summer festival, he added that this was a historic moment for the livelihoods and standards of living of the people of Mongolia and that his government aimed to distribute the country's natural wealth to the benefit of all.

"OT will play a significant role in our implementation of the Vision 2050 long-term policy," he said, explaining that the mine would help to more than double GDP per capita in the coming decade.

An elegant solution between trusted partners, as the two men declared. Music to the ears of many in the sector, but few enjoyed the rhythms of those inaugurative explosions more than Tserenbat Namsrai, CEO of Erdenes Oyu Tolgoi, or , or EOT, the state-owned firm that controls 34 percent of Oyu Tolgoi.

We meet at his office in downtown Ulaanbaatar. On a table by the window, glittering in the morning light, stands a copper plaque displaying Rio Tinto's commitment to cut the $2.4 billion debt. On the other side of the room, meanwhile, is a map of Mongolia showing the locations of all its mining projects, along with details of estimated deposits. In Tserenbat's mind, there will be several more sites plotted on the map.

"Here, look," he says, casting his arm over a vast area in the western part of the country. "There are many resources here: copper, gold, coal, rare earth minerals." His enthusiasm is like that of a kid in a candy store. There could be at least another five mining sites in Mongolia on a par with the OT project, he says.

"There are a lot of opportunities, as you can see. We have learned a lot from working with foreign investors through the Oyu Tolgoi project. Now, we are ready for the next mega mining agreement, where we again can find a win-win situation. We want to be a reliable and supportive partner and work with international quality investors."

He adds: "If we do things right, Mongolia becomes an Asian boom country. A very rich country."

He even has the numbers to back up his statement.

Between 2010 and 2022, the Oyu Tolgoi site generated a total of $3.9 billion for the Mongolian government, including value-added tax paid to local suppliers. According to estimates by EOT, royalties and taxes paid by Rio Tinto to the government will range between $100 and $300 million annually over the coming two decades, and will peak in 2030. Dividends paid to the government are expected to range between $400 and $700 million annually between 2037 and 2040, before declining to lower levels. Tserenbat stresses repeatedly that the numbers must be considered in the light of fluctuating commodity prices.

EOT's prognoses stretch to 2051, but geologists have estimated the mine may be in operation much longer, even until 2101. In total, the OT mine is expected to bank $13.4 billion for the Mongolian government between 2010 and 2051.

But, Tserenbat adds, this is "just money." The real value will not be calculated in monetary terms, he says, but in human terms.

"The major advantage from running high-quality mega mines, with the latest international technology, is that we get the know-how and people with world-standard skills," he says. "International inves-tors bring advanced technology and innovation to Mongolia. This mine—Oyu Tolgoi—is like a global benchmark, best practice, and the people who work here become among the best in the world in modern mining."

Several people I spoke to, both locals and foreigners, back up this statement and are quick to point out that skilled Mongolian mining staff—from blue-collar laborers to management—are key to the sector's future and its chances of rising up the value chain. Makes sense. Many people who have worked at Oyu Tolgoi are now in leading positions at other mining sites around the world, accord-ing to insiders I met.

A middle manager at a Canadian mining company tells me that his firm used to have more than 50 expats during the boom years, but that this figure now stands at no more than five. International firms in general need fewer foreign staff to run operations here, as local Mongolians have become increasingly skilled at what they do.

Echoing these statements, Orgil Sainkhuu, country manager for FLSmidth, the world's biggest manufacturer of mining processing technology, told me in an interview that the biggest source of value in the mining industry is always the same: people.

"If you have the right people, you can do anything," he said. "There will always be money available. The only thing that can stop a project is lack of people, and we are building up capacity with skilled people very fast in Mongolia now. We already have a very high education level, a high level of university graduates. Oyu Tolgoi, for example, is an absolutely world-class mine and processing plant, including the engineers, all hardworking people, and management. Absolutely world class."

Based in Copenhagen, Denmark, some 12,000 people employed in more than 60 countries, FLSmidth provides the global cement and mineral industries with factories, machinery, services, and know-how. In short, the company aims to help miners produce more using fewer resources and with a smaller footprint. In Mongolia, it is instrumental in many of the biggest mining projects, including Oyu Tolgoi.

From his corner office windows, Sainkhuu has a view of the Oyu Tolgoi headquarters in one direction and of a government building in the other. It's like he's keeping watch over the project's principal keyholders.

FLSmidth, which boasts on its website of a mission to reach net-zero emissions in mining and cement by 2030, recently signed a collaboration agreement with the Swedish-Swiss engineering giant ABB, also a big player in Mongolia, on pooling their resources and sharing expertise to improve environmental performance, safety, and productivity in mining. "If we can combine state-of-the-art equipment with digital solutions, we can better help customers achieve their business goals and carbon-free operations," a statement read.

The agreement is indicative of a broader trend in mining globally, and Mongolia does not lag behind; mining operators in the country are sharpening their focus on reducing environmental impacts and introducing sweeping measures to improve energy efficiency and waste management and to reduce carbon emissions. Rio Tinto, for example, has committed to completely decarbonizing its operations at Oyu Tolgoi. Such efforts require both innovative thinking about green solutions and lots of digitalization.

For its part, ABB, which has had a foothold in the country since 1932, told me about its commitments both to Mongolia and to transforming the industry.

"With further prospecting and exploration expected in Mongolia, we anticipate more discoveries and projects to happen over the next decades," said a spokesperson at the company's headquarters in Zurich, adding that ABB envisions converting existing mines from fossil fuel energy to all-electric as it strives toward establishing an energy-efficient, CO_2-free future.

"Together with our customers and partners, we help the mining industry meet its sustainability goals while staying competitive and ensuring high productivity, with our electrification, automation and digital solutions."

In light of such ambitions, Orgil Sainkhuu at FLSmidth has no doubt that better technology, and more skilled people will ultimately lead to a greener and more lucrative mining industry in Mongolia.

"The mining industry will become much more efficient going forward," he says. "The cost of production will go down; I'm very sure about that. Technology will be the key factor, with the right people implementing and the right people using it. Sustainability will also become much better."

He adds: "In Mongolia, the mining industry is *the* generator of dollars. The industry will continue—for a period of at least my lifetime, maybe the next generation's lifetime too—to be the most powerful contributor to the Mongolian economy and exports. Other sectors will grow bigger, too, but so will mining."

A generator of dollars

Orgil Sainkhuu is not the only one who sees mining as "*the* generator of dollars." Many reports have painted a picture of a mining country on the edge of renewed success, and investments in the sector are expected to bear fruit within a few short years.

The London-based consultancy firm CRU Group predicted in a 2021 outlook report that Mongolian mining will experience rapid growth until at least 2030. As investment is made to increase capacity, it's estimated that the copper and coal sectors specifically will "expand two times" in the current decade, according to a media report on CRU's findings.

Total income in the mining sector will increase from $5.3 billion to $12.5 billion, the report added. Dependency on mining will also increase, of course: if Mongolia's GDP grows by 5 percent annually, the mining sector's contribution will grow from 19.7 percent, as of 2020, to 32.7 percent by the year of 2030, estimates CRU.

"Not only does the country have some of the world's largest undeveloped copper, gold, and coal reserves, but it has many other undeveloped mineral deposits, in addition to being on the doorstep of the world's largest commodity consuming market," noted CRU China CEO John Johnson, a regular visitor to Mongolia over the last decade, in an earlier statement.

Fitch Solutions, a research agency, also offers a strong outlook on Mongolia's mining sector, based both on global demand and on the country's investments in infrastructure.

"Mongolia's mining sector growth will accelerate on the back of improving commodity prices, foreign mining investment, a robust infrastructure framework, and the market's strategic close proximity to major export markets such as mainland China. Projects such as Rio Tinto's Oyu Tolgoi mine will significantly increase the market's mining output over the coming years," Fitch observes in a 2023 report, although it also highlights that political risks could throw the forecasts off.

Let's look at the outlook for copper in particular. In short, copper is essential to modern life. It's used in everything from computer chips and toasters to power systems and air conditioners. The metal, considered the optimal conductor of electricity, is also key to a greener world. Electric vehicles use more than twice as much copper as gasoline-powered cars, according to the International Copper Alliance, a trade association. Both demand and prices are likely to skyrocket going forward, according to many reports.

As the world goes electric, net-zero emission goals will double demand for copper to 50 million metric tons annually by 2035, according to an industry-funded study from S&P Global. While that forecast is largely hypothetical given that such an amount of copper can't be consumed if it isn't available, other analyses also point to the potential for a surge. Bloomberg NEF, a research provider covering global commodity markets, estimates that demand will increase by more than 50 percent from 2022 to 2040.

Meanwhile, as alluded to, there's not enough supply to meet this demand. In fact, the world could be headed toward a historic copper deficit of up to 10 million tons in 2035, according to S&P Global.

"The challenges this poses are reminiscent of the 20th-century scramble for oil but may be accentuated by an even higher geographic concentration for copper resources and the downstream industry to refine it into products," notes the report.

It adds: "Unless massive new supply comes online in a timely way, the goal of Net-Zero Emissions by 2050 will be short-circuited and remain out of reach."

This will have an immense effect on prices. As with all commodities, price fluctuations are a constant headache. A dramatic fall in the price of copper in the first part of 2022, for example, made investors nervous despite the metal's strong long-term outlook.

"We'll look back at 2022 and think, 'oops,'" said John LaForge, head of real asset strategy at Wells Fargo, in an interview with

Bloomberg. "The market is just reflecting the immediate concerns. But if you really think about the future, you can see the world is clearly changing. It's going to be electrified, and it's going to need a lot of copper."

Even if demand is global, China is the key player. The Asian economic powerhouse consumes more than half of the world's copper output.

Coal—controversial as it may be—is also on the upswing. Coal is, of course, one of Mongolia's biggest earners, having average exports of around 1,300 trucks of the fossil fuel a day, according to local media sources. Mongolia has emerged as the top supplier of coking coal to China, where it's used in the production of steel, in the absence of Australian coal (due to a diplomatic feud between Beijing and Canberra).

Coking coal, or metallurgical coal, is a grade of coal that can be used to produce high-quality coke, an essential fuel in the steel-making process. Mongolian coal tends currently to be used more by steelmakers than by power plants. Due to growing electricity demand, however, power plants in China are expected to consume ever greater amounts of coal in the coming years—and according to several reports it just keeps building new coal plants. "Mongolia's coal exports to China are expected to rise further in the near term," according to the investment bank Founder Cifco.

However, sales of coal and other fossil fuels are coming under increasing international scrutiny. "Demand for key minerals is likely to tumble due to climate change concerns, a shift of investors' preference toward sustainability, [and] China's ambitious goal to reduce coal consumption," the World Bank noted in a 2020 report about Mongolia's mining sector. It's also increasingly difficult to get funding from investment firms and international institutions for projects connected to coal. The current global energy crisis in the wake of the war in Ukraine has accelerated the shift to renewable energy, and renewables are expected to surpass coal power by 2027, according to a 2022 International Energy Agency forecast. A post-fossil fuel world is coming at us faster than we think.

Yet—for now at least—coal is king in Mongolia.

Let's also look at one more key ingredient for today's world: rare earth metals. These are used to manufacture everything from electric cars, missiles, and wind turbines to iPhones and flat-screen televisions, demand expected to keep increasing over the coming decade.

Mongolia is home to major deposits of rare-earth minerals. According to a 2009 survey by US government geologists, Mongolia sits on 31 million tons of rare earth resources, which was equal to 16.8 percent of known reserves worldwide at the time and makes Mongolia the second-biggest source globally after China. The minerals are relatively common worldwide, but it is hard to find a whole suite of them in one place, and even with the best will in the world from mining corporations, it is extremely difficult to extract them without damaging the environment.

What's more, the metals are also a potential weapon in the escalating tech war and geopolitical feud between Beijing and Washington.

"If China was to stop exporting this it would be a big problem for the US, at least in the short term," Allan von Mehren, chief analyst at Danske Bank in Copenhagen, told me in an interview a few years ago. "China holds a trump card in the near-monopoly of rare earth minerals."

It would not be the first time China had disrupted global trade in such minerals. In late 2010, Beijing cut Japan off temporarily from rare-earths after an unrelated dispute over fishing rights.

From this perspective, non-aligned Mongolia would be a welcome player on the global market.

Already, adventurous geologists and international exploration firms are sniffing around to find the next Mongolian subsoil treasure trove.

"The Oyu Tolgoi mine has become a symbol of Mongolia's potential as a mineral-rich province and just like the proverbial light globe that attracts the moths, Oyu Tolgoi has attracted a band of smaller capped hopefuls to the region in search of its sister deposit that many believe may still be lurking out in the Mongolian desert somewhere," the *West Australian* wrote recently.

Meanwhile, international leaders have become alert to Mongolia's potential as a source of much-needed minerals for the renewable energy sector. When German Chancellor Olaf Scholz welcomed Mongolian Prime Minister Oyun-Erdene to Berlin in October 2022, he said Mongolia would be "an important partner" for "many raw materials" in Germany's diversification strategy.

Several reports focus on the vast potential for international firms to invest in Mongolian mining, while also highlighting that frail investment laws and potential government interventions pose challenges for the sector.

"Mongolia's economy and mining sector hold immense potential for investors looking to leverage the country's abundant mineral resources and rapidly growing economy," notes the Hong Kong-based consultancy firm Dezan Shira & Associates in a 2023 China Briefing newsletter. "Although there are some obstacles, such as political instability and infrastructure limitations, the government's dedication to encouraging foreign investment and enhancing the investment environment, combined with the nation's ample natural resources and strategic position, make it an appealing investment destination."

Uyanga Bold holds a PhD from the Department of Earth and Planetary Sciences at Harvard University and is head of the Geology Policy Department at Mongolia's Ministry of Mining and Heavy Industry. She explains that large swaths of the country have not yet been studied for subsoil resources, indicating huge potential for new large-scale findings.

"Our department is working to understand subsoil Mongolia in more detail, using modern technologies," she tells me during an interview at a small, noisy café called Millie's Espresso in Ulaanbaatar. "We're collaborating with scientists from around the world. We need to study the region more closely to find a suitable environment and to find the next Oyu Tolgoi."

She refers to the Fraser Institute's annual survey on mining economies, a key source for international investors when making decisions. In 2021, it scored Mongolia high in potential deposits but lower on mining regulations and transparency. The governance results were echoed in another survey by the Natural Resource Governance Index.

"The most important factor in any scoring system is the mineral potential index, at least for me as a geologist," says Uyanga. "And there are potentials for new mining projects to be found in Mongolia. We need to be smart about doing basic geological research work and pointing to the right places."

With a wry smile, she adds: "Luckily, I'm in charge of the mineral potential part [and not the political part]."

This is OT ... this is OT ... this is OT

The fine line between mineral miracle and resource curse is ever-present in Mongolia in general. But it becomes all the more strikingly evident when visiting Khanbogd, a village next to the Oyu Tolgoi site in Umnugobi province.

This tranquil community is entirely contingent on the mine, and on the goodwill of Rio Tinto. Most families who live here make their living, directly or indirectly, from the mine, and much of the infrastructure and public services—roads, a school, a hospital, the town square, etcetera—are financed by the company. Some public workers, including schoolteachers, are even partly supported by it. At the time of my visit, the mining company shared an office building with the local government. Determining who actually calls the shots here is not straightforward.

As we drive through the village, careful not to disturb the camels that roam some of its thoroughfares, a representative for the mining company points to different buildings and facilities financed by the firm. Her commentary approximates something like a looped announcement: "This is OT ... this is OT ... this is OT ..." It almost becomes comical. Even in the restaurant where we have lunch there are large photographs of the mining site on the walls, the rep proudly declaring: "See, that's OT." Point taken.

Compared to other administrative districts or *sums*, however, Khanbogd is relatively rich. Most other villages receive financial support from the central government, while, according to the politicians I speak with, this frontier-like outpost is financially self-reliant and actually sends money in the other direction, to Ulaanbaatar. The economic impact of Oyu Tolgoi is visible on the streets: it has more grocery stores, restaurants, and karaoke bars than most other villages. Around 4,000 people live here, some in residential buildings and others in traditional nomadic *gers*, thousands of camels and cashmere goats roaming the surrounding countryside. Many of the workers here reportedly make more money and enjoy higher living standards than does the governor.

"Life is good here," says Tavanjin Buyan-Ulzii, chairman of the local Citizens' Representatives assembly and a former governor of Khanbogd. "You can't compare this place to other *sums* or rural areas in Mongolia."

He has been part of Khanbogd's story since the first explorers and geologists came here to dig two decades ago. Back then, the rural economy was dominated by livestock. Its development since, driven by investment connected to the mining site, has rarely been free of complications: herders have filed a number of legal complaints about a lack of financial compensation and concerns over water shortages and a river diversion. Access to water remains a concern today and is the local government's "number one priority," according to Tavanjin Buyan-Ulzii.

When asked if he's worried about the dependency on one single commercial company, he doesn't hesitate: "Of course. But we keep developing our local economy into new sectors. We have more camels than any village in Mongolia. We are also close to the Chinese border and are investing in tourism for people to come here and enjoy the natural beauty. The development is future-oriented."

From this perspective, the little village of Khanbogd serves as an illustration of how angels and demons often appear to loom side by side over the country's mining sector, sometimes at loggerheads. It demonstrates how subsoil riches can shape a whole society, bringing wealth and promise but also alarming reminders of the need for balanced finances, economic diversification, and sustainability.

Meanwhile, as politicians, development bankers, management consultants and company executives struggle to find the perfect formula for the industry, drivers of yellow mining trucks, like Dugaraa, will continue to bring excavated soil up from the hole in the ground at Oyu Tolgoi to be processed and transported to China, day in and day out, for decades to come. And some of the truck drivers will continue to toss tea into the sky as an offering to the spirits for good karma. Perhaps it would be a good idea for government officials, industry leaders, and international investors to do the same.

3

Silicon steppe: A green tech giant stirs

> *A new generation of Mongolian tech entrepreneurs is pow-ering change, embracing "nomadic tech," and forging a renewable energy future for Asia.*

Tears flow down the cheeks of a teenage girl as she pulls her gaze away from the stage. "I'm happy, but we worked so hard," she sobs softly. "I wish our project had won."

It's the final ceremony of a two month-long coding bootcamp for Mongolian girls, many of them from underprivileged backgrounds or nomadic families far away from the capital. We are in a ballroom at a five-star hotel in downtown Ulaanbaatar, and the staff are serving wine to the adults and soft drinks to the youngsters, together with finger food and pastries. The room buzzes with excitement. The girls—all wearing white T-shirts emblazoned with the hacking program's "Girls </> Code" logo—are charged up to the max after an evening spent presenting their team projects to an audience of tech industry heavyweights, government officials, and foreign diplomats.

The projects themselves range from travel sites and online games to a smart emergency-alert system for women, all conceived and coded during eight weeks of the summer holidays. None of the girls had any coding experience before joining the program, and as they presented their work, each project seemed more impressive than the last. Together, they point the way to a new generation of female technology leaders in Mongolia.

"You're the future, you're the powerhouse, you're the engine of change," says Tapan Mishra, resident coordinator for the UN in Mongolia, in a closing speech. "You are ready for the world. You are ready to open new doors and new windows, for your own careers, but also to make sure that Mongolian girls are noticed in the world. You can really matter. You will lead Mongolia to what it needs to become."

Several of the girls I meet express confidence that they are indeed ready for the world—and ready to pursue their dreams of a future in tech.

"I want to continue with coding . . . I want to go to the United States and study software engineering at MIT," says 18-year-old Enkhzul, referring to the prestigious Massachusetts Institute of Technology.

Together with her FPG (Future Programmer Girls) teammates Byambajargal, Batzul, and Davaajargal, Enkzhul has spent the program developing an online game that combines Mongolian horse racing and *shagai* (a kind of dice traditionally made from the ankle bones of sheep). After their presentation, the girls tour the room, allowing guests—including the CEOs of some of the country's largest telecom and technology firms—to try out their game on a laptop. It's fun and simple—and surprisingly intuitive to play.

When asked if she would like to stay in the US after her studies and pursue a career at one of the tech giants, Enkhzul's answer comes without hesitation: "No, not at all. I want to go back to Mongolia and use my skills and work with tech here. One day, I'd like to start my own company and spread information about our culture. I want my company to be a world-famous Mongolian brand."

Of the thousands of girls who applied for the Girls for Coding program, 50 were admitted in 2022 through a three-stage selection process. Those 50 then received hundreds of hours of tailor-made training in coding, delivered by tutors from the School of Applied Science and Engineering at the National University of Mongolia. IT and finance industry executives also visited the camp to share their experience and insights.

For many of those participating, the closing ceremony was an emotional roller-coaster, the whole evening a culmination of two months of hard work and dedication, sleepless nights, computers breaking down just days before deadline, and general frustrations of the sort only understood by coders. One could feel how a sense of sisterhood had formed among the girls. After their presentations, the excitement turned to relief, and finally deflation, as it suddenly dawned on them that two months of blood, sweat, tears, and toil had come to an end. It was time to go home. Tears sprang quickly to many a tired young eye.

The ceremony was also attended by a cohort of girls from the previous year. "I remember the feeling," one of them told me. "Saying goodbye to everyone but also a feeling of almost mentally collapsing because the camp and hard work was over and the projects were finished."

She added that the program had helped her grow as a person. "Before joining the bootcamp, I didn't have much self-confidence. I didn't think I could do it or speak to strangers. But I did do it, and I'm a much more confident woman today. Perhaps that was the most important win for me, perhaps even more important than learning to code."

The program was initiated by Bolor-Erdene Battsengel, one of Mongolia's most widely known tech personalities and a woman recognized as much for her sense of style as for having driven a revolution in public services for the digital age. The coding girls refer to her as "sister," a reverential title. Tapan Mishra from the UN calls her "a global icon" and says she's proof that "Mongolian women can make waves in the world."

In essence, Bolor-Erdene started Girls for Coding to sow the seeds of a digital future for Mongolia by making space for women in tech.

"I'm so proud of the girls; they are all fantastic," she tells me in an interview. "I wish I could expand the program to the whole world. I try to give the girls opportunities. I'm not forcing them to become software engineers, but I'm giving them opportunities to see the options are there to become a software engineer or work in tech."

Her overall aim is to transform Mongolia into a "digital first" country. In Mongolia, women generally have a higher level of education than men do, but they lag behind in IT participation. The Girls for Coding program was launched to try to flatten gender inequality in the field and to redress regional divisions in the country. A number of the girls from previous years have gone on to be accepted to prestigious universities in the US and the UK.

Empowering young women is essential to achieving sustainable economic development, according to The World Bank. A 2023 outlook report stated that Mongolia would benefit from more inclusive job creation and called for rising labor force participation among women and better opportunities for young people in general. Despite the fact that, as mentioned, Mongolian women are better educated than are their male peers and that literacy rates are higher among women, they are also less likely to make use of this education.

Initiatives such as the girls' coding bootcamp, and an emerging tech start-up scene that has a more inclusive outlook, are welcomed as steps forward.

Bolor-Erdene's own background is not much different from that of many of the bootcamp girls. She grew up in Bulgan province, in the northern part of Mongolia. She excelled in mathematics in school and had a knack for computers, but many of her teachers discouraged her from pursuing higher education or a career in tech. Instead, they recommended more "female" professions such as admin. Bolor-Erdene, however, had different plans.

Over the years, hard work and a passion for social development took her from a rural town on the Mongolian steppe to the center of government. At 14, she graduated from high school, and at 18 she finished college and went on to the University of Oxford, where she studied public policy. She has ten years of experience in international development working with the UN, the World Bank, and the Asian Development Bank.

At the age of 29, she became vice minister in Mongolia's Ministry of Digital Development and Communications, becoming the youngest person ever to attain such a level of seniority in Mongolian politics. In 2021, she was selected by Forbes in its "30 under 30" list of the world's brightest young things. The Trend Spotter, a fashion and lifestyle website, wrote that Bolor-Erdene carves out her own way and brings youth and beauty to Mongolia's government. Overall, she has come to epitomize a new generation of government officials whose experience and mindset is international—she's very much one of Prime Minister Luvsannamsrai Oyun-Erdene's *padawans*, as explained in Chapter 1. In 2022, as I was researching this book, Bolor-Erdene left her ministerial position to complete a policy fellowship at Oxford University, but she's still running the Girls for Coding program and pushing for digitalization in the country.

Her office in the ministry, right across the street from the Government Palace, looked different from many other ministerial offices I've visited: it was more stylish, and full of light, with minimalistic design details. On her desk she had a cup of green tea, an open bar of chocolate, documents in neatly organized folders, and a pile of books, including *The ABCs of AOC* by the American politician and activist Alexandria Ocasio-Cortez; *The Phoenix Project*, a novel about how to succeed in tech and business; and *The Spirit of Democracy*, a book by the social scientist Larry Diamond about the struggle to build free societies.

Political careers are rarely a bed of roses—far from it. But being a young woman in a male-dominated environment such as the Mongolian state brings some unique challenges. Bolor-Erdene regaled me with a string of anecdotes, equal parts comical and disconcerting. When *Time* magazine ran a profile of her in its issue on "Next Generation Leaders," this is how the story opened:

In 2020, when Bolor-Erdene Battsengel would walk into work in Ulaanbaatar's national parliament building, security guards would stop her to ask if she was a personal assistant or a janitor. She was neither—she was the youngest member of the Mongolian government's Cabinet, appointed to help lead the nation's digital transformation.

When I bring it up, she laughs dryly at the memory of attending the chamber as head of the Communication and Information Technology Department, a policymaking government body, at the age of 27.

"The security guards were asking, like, 'Who are you? Why are you here?' And I said, 'I'm here for the Cabinet session.' And they were like, 'Are you here for a waitress job? Are you assistant to a Parliament member?'"

She recalls that, whenever she rose to her feet to talk about her plans to digitalize and modernize the nation, eyebrows would also shoot up among Cabinet members. Furthermore, harassment was not uncommon, even from female colleagues. On one occasion, an older female colleague at the ministry offered some advice as to how Bolor-Erdene might fit in better: "Eat more and get fat; then they'll respect you." Disappointing, for all the obvious reasons. More generally, Bolor-Erdene's energetic and entrepreneurial "Yes we can!" attitude ruffled lots of feathers.

"When I joined the government, it was a very traditional institution, like everywhere in the world," she says. "You can't just bring a start-up leadership style to government. I think I kind of turned out to be very aggressive, to be honest, and very into detail, but also I don't like the bureaucracy and the levels within the government."

She adds: "It became clear that I had to work extra hard to be accepted for who I am."

Today, it's fair to say she has earned her stripes—in tandem with the digitalization ministry itself. Bolor-Erdene has been a crucial driver in transforming a nomad society into a digital nation. In October 2020, her team launched the e-Mongolia platform, which has digitalized hundreds of government services and made it easier for Mongolians to register a company, order a new passport, or get a driver's license. Previously, people in the countryside would have to travel for hours, even days, to visit the city to conduct simple administrative tasks; today they can do it on their mobile phones. This is vital in a country as vast as Mongolia.

In short, the goals of the platform are to reduce bureaucracy and duplication of work by government organizations and to counter citizens' frustrations at inefficient public services (something people crave in most countries, perhaps). For inspiration, Mongolia took lessons from Estonia's e-platform, which has allowed that Baltic nation's various public and private sector e-service information systems to link up and function in harmony. Ulaanbaatar and Tallinn today have a close tech partnership, and e-Mongolia is used by nearly everyone in the land.

"You can actually see a herder on a horse in the wilderness of Mongolia using a smartphone and getting government services," Bolor-Erdene says with a smile. (It's a claim that I'm able to verify when I speak to nomadic herders, far from the capital, who are full of praise for e-Mongolia and the ease with which it allows them to interact with different government bodies. More about these "digital nomads" in Chapter 4.)

During our interview at her office, Bolor-Erdene points to a large digital screen opposite her desk that monitors e-Mongolia usage around the country in real time. Small green and yellow dots fly across the screen, representing individual interactions with the service.

Besides e-Mongolia, the ministry has initiated a national digital literacy program, focused mainly on target groups such as herders, elderly people, and disadvantaged people. This is important, Bolor-Erdene says, because "the new inequality is digital exclusion." At the same time, various new laws have been passed, covering open data-sharing, personal data protection, cyber security, digital signatures, and digital assets. Now, if a government employee checks a citizen's data for any purpose, the citizen gets a notification. It's 100 percent transparent, explains Bolor-Erdene. How many other countries have that same level of transparency toward citizens, one might wonder.

The e-Mongolia platform has gained global recognition, and other governments are now reaching out to the digitalization ministry here to learn how they can create similar systems and streamline their own public service delivery.

"When I go abroad and give speeches about tech in Mongolia or the e-Mongolia platform to international audiences, they are often shocked at first, like 'Can this really be from Mongolia?'" Bolor-Erdene says. "For many people, even the educated, the image they have of Mongolia is mostly of mining or horses."

She adds: "I usually get very positive comments from the international community, especially from leaders from more developed countries, because they don't expect to see Mongolia having e-governance that is better than in their own countries. We get requests from other countries to learn from e-Mongolia's experience, which is encouraging."

Her achievements haven't gone unnoticed at home either. One morning as we were having coffee at a downtown restaurant, a young waiter walked up to her. "I just want to say that I support what you do very much," he said, blushing fiercely. "I'm a big fan."

Mongolia's plans for digitalization go way beyond the delivery of public services through an app, however. Bolor-Erdene explains that Mongolia wants to become a digital nation as part of a wider push to diversify its economy, as outlined in its New Recovery Policy and Vision 2050 roadmaps. As part of this push, the government is currently working on creating an ICT Free Zone, which it hopes will simultaneously boost local firms and attract foreign companies. The essence of free zones is low or no taxation, but they also encourage specific industries to cluster around a physical location. In Mongolia's case, Khushigtiin Khundii, also known as Maidar City, is being planned as a new, eco-friendly city south of Ulaanbaatar. The government will lead by example by moving various departments there, including the Ministry of Digital Development and Communications.

"The ICT Free Zone is about creating that friendlier environment for IT firms, start-ups in particular, while also supporting local Mongolian companies," Bolor-Erdene says.

Her role, as she sees it, is not just to roll out digitalization in the country and attract investment but to spread the word about its start-ups and ICT champions to the wider world. On many occasions, she has taken Mongolian start-up founders to international events and conferences—some attended by luminaries such as Meta's Mark Zuckerberg or members of the Saudi royal family—and facilitated introductions to foreign investors and tech executives. And she's not shy of boasting about her Mongolian tech darlings.

"I always tell people that Mongolia is a hidden gem," she says. "It is a hidden technology gem that is booming now. Investors need to get in early to find the best opportunities, so what I am telling people is to come and take a look, check us out."

She adds: "Our economy used to be all about mining. Technology offers Mongolia a second chance. That's what I am working to achieve."

Echoing her words, Gantumur Luvsannyam, leader of the country's opposition Democratic Party and a former minister for Education and Science, sees great potential in Mongolia's future as an innovation hub. For the country to reach its potential in this area, his party argues for more liberal reforms and tax cuts to attract foreign direct investments. He also wants to create more free-trade zones and science parks.

"We want to lower taxes so money instead will go to research and development," he tells me in an interview. "My vision of Mongolia is that we become a science-based country. We must strive to become the 'Silicon Steppe.'"

An Asian hub of innovation

Mongolia's is a relatively young tech start-up scene that has accelerated in substance and visibility over the last few years. A lack of deep-pocketed investors has long been a hurdle, as is the case in many other developing regions, but more recently local and international financiers have been throwing increasingly large amounts of money at the sector, according to several people I speak to. This is partly because of the commercial appeal of individual firms but also because of good old FOMO: fear of missing out. Some people have even said the country is facing a "new boom era" based on tech. Something is happening, no question.

"The Silicon Valley vibe started spreading in Mongolia since about 2010," writes Ider-Od Bat-Erdene, co-founder of the advertisement solutions provider CallPro, in a blog post. "Before that, names like Google, Amazon, and Intuit always sounded way too distant and foreign to talk much about. However, now one can bump into armies of energetic young entrepreneurs at events such as Start-up Weekend, Start-up Grind, and Start-up Next at IT Park, a state-run incubator, in downtown Ulaanbaatar. . . . The start-up scene in Mongolia is starting to shine for investors."

The Hong Kong-based business management consultancy firm Dezan Shira & Associates believes it's high time that investors recognized Mongolia's transition from mines to minds.

In a 2022 article by one of the firm's partners, Enkhzul Orgodol, she wrote: "For the past decade, the Mongolian mining sector has been at the center of foreign investors' attention and national export goals. Yet, for the past few years, a different sector has been gaining as much or even more popularity and attraction among both the locals and the internationals." She continued: "With the global rise of Web 3.0, educated youth driving digital transformation and [an] internal push for developing non-mining related sectors, Mongolia has made concrete steps forward in leveling up its game in the digital business sector."

Certainly, over the last few years Mongolia and Ulaanbaatar have climbed in global tech start-up rankings although they do have a long way to go to compete with other Asian start-up hubs such as Shenzhen, Singapore, and Seoul. The country is also increasingly punching above its weight in international innovation rankings.

In StartupBlink's 2022 Global Rankings Report, Mongolia jumped seven places to rank 81st in the world (22 positions higher than in 2020, the first year the country was included). The country ranked 14th in Asia. Ulaanbaatar, meanwhile, was the seventh highest-ranking non-Chinese city in the Central Asia Regional Economic Cooperation business region.

Not too bad for a country mostly known for mines and horses.

I reached out to Eli David, the co-founder and CEO of StartupBlink, the Israeli-based start-up research center, to get his view on Mongolia. "I'm very optimistic about the future of Mongolia's tech start-up scene," he said in an online call from Haifa. "Mongolia's scene started late, and they are fighting against the wind. But if they keep pushing, they can create a good ecosystem for the future."

The report ranks the start-up ecosystems of 100 countries and 1,000 cities with the help of an algorithm that weighs the quality and quantity of start-ups, their sponsors, and the overall business environment. The research firm's data indicates that both tech talent and the number of high-quality start-ups in Mongolia have enjoyed significant spikes and that the country's emerging IT sector is leading the economy in a radical new direction. It affirms that Ulaanbaatar has the potential to become "an Asian hub of innovation."

"Most people know Mongolia for its nature and unique nomadic history, but the quality of Mongolian startups might soon make the country famous for its innovation as well," StartupBlink's report notes. "Mongolia's start-up ecosystem is still developing, but it has the potential to greatly impact and transform the local economy. A surge in investment in human capital and digital connectivity offers an opportunity for this East Asian country to fortify its gains from agriculture and mining and take advantage of the demand for IT to create a start-up ecosystem in its capital city, Ulaanbaatar."

The Israeli firm specifically highlights the e-Mongolia platform and its consolidation during the pandemic. While Mongolia's digital revolution began before COVID-19, the health crisis helped to accelerate the process. And while the government's reforms were primarily aimed at reducing bureaucracy, improving transparency, and offering more responsive services, there has been the added effect, StartupBlink believes, of benefitting the start-up scene. Noting that other initiatives—including the Science Industry Innovation Agency of Ulaanbaatar City, Startup Mongolia (an NGO that offers resources and networking opportunities), and the Youth Business Mongolia program—have also helped, the firm adds that it's "encouraging to see events such as Startup 2022 and Startup Week Ulaanbaatar take place. [The] ecosystem is maturing."

In other rankings, the 2021 Global Innovation Index placed Mongolia at 58th place among more than 200 countries and regions, and 5th among countries with a "small or average economy." The rankings were jointly compiled by the UN's World Intellectual Property Organization, the European business school INSEAD, and

America's Cornell University. The researchers said that considering Mongolia's GDP and level of development, its ranking was "above expectations."

Despite its small population, the country is certainly not short of talent. It produces some 50,000 IT graduates each year and runs several coding and software development programs. The country's proficiency in math is another plus. In 2021, Mongolia ranked 11th in the International Mathematical Olympiad, far ahead of teams from developed countries such as Finland or Norway, and up from 50th place in 2010.

Clearly, Mongolia is getting a lot right, but, again, it still has a long way to go to catch up with other leading start-up and innovation hubs. Growth in the country's start-up ecosystem continues to face obstacles both in relation to physical infrastructure and access to finance.

"Mongolia is a small market," Eli David said. "Therefore, it's important that Mongolian tech firms think like companies in Israel, Sweden, or Estonia and not focus only on their home market. They should think global from day one."

One of the biggest challenges facing Mongolia's tech sector, he added, is that most people around the world are not aware of it, while also having an outdated view of the country in general. Bol-or-Erdene called the technology sector a "hidden gem," but for many international investors, leaders, and businesspeople it's the first word in that phrase that remains the operative one.

"Perception is a big problem," David said. "I don't think Mongolia suffers from a bad image, but its image is definitely not a place you would expect to find cutting-edge tech start-ups, and that is what has to be fixed."

"Did you ride in on a horse?"

This phenomenon of people abroad still being shocked or surprised, or even skeptical, when they hear about Mongolian tech is something I learn of repeatedly, not least from tech start-up entrepreneurs who have experience of pitching to international investors.

One person who knows a thing or two about Mongolia's less-than-stellar reputation in innovation and IT, and about some investors' unfavorable views, is the country's most famous tech start-up entrepreneur, Anar Chinbaatar.

"Once I had a meeting with an investor in a country in Asia, and when he realized I was from Mongolia it was like he was thinking, 'Oh, did you ride in on a horse? Where do you stay, in a tent on the parking lot?'" Chinbaatar tells me wryly, adding: "He was such an idiot, it was so annoying."

Bad luck for the investor. Chinbaatar's group of companies today have business interests (and other investors) not only in Mongolia but across Asia and in Silicon Valley, and he's looking to reach unicorn status—which denotes a start-up with a valuation of at least $1 billion. Oh, and one more thing: he's planning to build a hotel. In space. Yes, you read that right.

Having some 20 start-ups under his belt, Chinbaatar and his partners' biggest creations to date are AND Global—a cutting-edge fintech company and the owner of Mongolia's leading micro-loan service provider, LendMN—and ONDO, a mobile operator that is piloting the latest generation of high-speed mobile internet and 5G technologies in the country. The group is also setting up a satellite branch in the San Francisco Bay Area to expand into the US and other international markets. ("*And*" means "best friend" in Mongolian, and "*Ondo*" means "unique.")

Before our first meeting, someone explained to me that "Anar is like Mongolia's Steve Jobs, just much wilder." The truth is not far off. The first time we meet is at a flashy Japanese restaurant in the Shangri-La complex. His hair is all over the place, his eyes attentive, and the conversation rattles off on one speed: full speed. As we gulp down tempura and sushi, the discussion jumps from his adventures in the start-up world and his love of mathematics to *real* adventures in motorcycle racing, including the Dakar Rally, and various other outdoor daredevil escapades. The motorcycle magazine *Canada Moto Guide* wrote in 2016 that his performance in the Dakar Rally was a "unique effort," explaining that "Anar Chinbaatar showed up from Mongolia and managed to finish what was essentially his first major motorcycle race—which is a better result than plenty of more famous riders."

"Whenever I need to recharge myself, I just ride on my bike and go in any direction for days," he says.

In case you are wondering: yes, this is the same person who grew up in the town of Berkh, fighting off a drunk miner side by side with the current prime minister when they were young boys, as explained in the introduction to this book. "It's a horrible story," he remembers.

Considering his lifestyle, it's certainly understandable that Chinbaatar needs to recharge every now and then. He has dark rings under his eyes, bearing witness to many years glued to screens. He explains that he has lately cut down on his working hours, from 100 hours a week to "only" 80, adding (half-jokingly) that occasionally he can now see his wife in "natural daylight" for the first time in years. When he again, half-jokingly, asserts that he would never employ anyone without rings under their eyes, which he takes as a sign of commitment, it's hard not to believe him. In a famed TED talk video, Chinbaatar dares people to push themselves harder, to challenge themselves every day, to grow and find individual success. He's also one of the "sharks" in the local version of the American business reality television series *Shark Tank*. Undeniably, he's the stereotype of a hardworking start-up entrepreneur.

Throughout his career, Chinbaatar has sailed against the wind. As he tells it, local politicians, businesspeople, investors, and others have tried to keep him and his colleagues down—either because they haven't understood or believed in him, or because they've seen him as an unwanted competitor.

Conversely, this resistance has been the key to his group's success. The reason they started the lending platform LendMN themselves, in 2016, was through necessity, that time-honored mother of invention. Chinbaatar and his partners—all math geeks—had created an algorithm and software system that could predict and monitor repayments from microloans. But few people in business or finance, either in Mongolia or elsewhere, believed in or were willing to take a chance on them. Some local bank managers even brushed them off as scamsters. So, partly to prove everyone wrong, they decided to set up their own microlending platform. What better way to demonstrate that their technology worked?

They eventually managed to raise $4 million from backers in Mongolia and Japan—and the platform was an immediate success. Within a few short months it had disbursed hundreds of thousands of loans to people all across Mongolia, its loan model having proven instantly more appealing than traditional alternatives. The business turned a profit within two months of its commercial launch.

Their act of disruption didn't go unnoticed. In 2018, *Asiamoney* wrote, "Anar Chinbaatar is wreaking havoc: local banks are running scared of LendMN." The business website compared his story to

Travis Kalanick founding Uber and Mark Zuckerberg's creation of Facebook—and warned investors not to bet against him.

"When we launched, all the Mongolian banks had an emergency meeting over the weekend about how to tax or block us," Chinbaatar told *Forbes* one year after launch, adding that it turned out to be good for both competition and innovation in the sector. "Right after that, a lot of banks started working on new products, creating innovation departments to work on Facebook and chatbots."

Today, LendMN is listed on the Ulaanbaatar stock exchange—a defensive maneuver to make it harder for regulators to shut the platform down—and is the leading fintech platform in Mongolia, offering both microloans and a digital wallet that enables customers to make various types of payments and financial transactions. The parent company, AND Global, now also sells its machine learning-based SaaS lending system to banks and investors around the world and is developing other new artificial intelligence-powered financial products and services. It has offices in Ulaanbaatar, Tokyo, Manila, Yangon, Singapore, and Silicon Valley. The firm works in close collaboration with strategic investors based in Japan (Marubeni Corporation and SBI Holdings) and is headquartered in Singapore. In fact, international media have sometimes referred to it as a Singaporean company, but most of its employees are in Ulaanbaatar. According to Chinbaatar, AND Global is today valued at $65 million, while ONDO—which is registered in the US state of Delaware and is in the process of rolling out 5G IoT (Internet of Things) communication solutions internationally—is valued at $100 million.

Although Anar Chinbaatar comes across as confident and carefree, and constantly jokes about this and that, there's also a deeper seriousness about him. Behind his smiles and observant eyes, something melancholic lurks. It's as though, despite his success and fame, he's still unsatisfied and feels there's more to achieve—for himself and his businesses but also for his country. During our conversation, he often comes back to Mongolia's potential as a tech hub. He might be a tech guy, but his energy and drive seem to come from a deeper and more old-fashioned place: love of country.

Indeed, aside from expanding his own company, Chinbaatar has a bigger vision to rebrand Mongolia, allowing it to break from the shadows of its legendary emperor and the centuries-old nomadic culture that remains its abiding image.

"In Mongolia, we only have one brand—Chinggis Khan—and it's over 800 years old," he says, adding that the country needs fresh thinking to create international companies, brands, and whole industries. "All Mongolians are proud of our heritage, of Chinggis Khan, but often lack the confidence to create new global brands. It's holding our nation back. I would like to change the mindset among the younger generation."

Chinbaatar is the sponsor of several projects and NGOs aimed at nurturing the next generation of tech entrepreneurs—including the Girls for Coding program. He hopes the success of his businesses, and their expansion to the US and elsewhere, can serve as inspiration to young Mongolians. He also wants local investors to take lessons.

"My message to Mongolian investors is that you have to trust in the younger generation and in technology," he says. "That's partly why I agreed to be an investor in the TV show *Shark Tank*. They approached me and I said, 'I'm not a shark; I'm always fundraising.' But I agreed because I want to send a message to society, to investors."

There's a level of frustration in Chinbaatar's voice when talking about Mongolia's tech and investment environment—and about how much of his time is spent not in engineering or product development but in wining and dining politicians, businessmen, and other influential figures who want a piece of him and his fame. ("Drinking vodka, going blah blah blah, me acting like a clown," he says with a sigh.) He adds that inefficiency, political turbulence, corruption, and other bottlenecks remain systemic.

"Sometimes it feels like driving a Lamborghini in Berkh," he says, referring to the mining town where he grew up and where the roads are often unpaved and full of holes. "The car can go very fast, but the locals will say, 'Show us, in the dirt, how fast you can go.'"

The decision to try and gain a foothold in the US by establishing a presence in the San Francisco Bay Area was partly motivated by these frustrations. There, Chinbaatar and his partners will try to put the Lamborghini on the highway.

Their new company, under the ONDO umbrella, is called Andorean. Its purpose is to build a platform capable of integrating artificial intelligence across various industries, from smart city development to mining, by using private 5G networks and digital twin technology to monitor and control operations remotely.

"For me, what we are doing is trying to build a Mongolian-origin, globally known brand. It will also be an opportunity for Mongolians living in the US to join our vision." Chinbaatar himself plans to split his time between San Francisco and Ulaanbaatar.

Nami Bold, head of Andorean in the US, says that setting up the new entity is a way to "unchain" the group from the problems of corruption and insufficient investment in Mongolia and unlock its international potential.

Over lunch at a vegan restaurant—of which there are several in downtown Ulaanbaatar nowadays—she lays out her visions both for the company and for herself. Nami is among those Mongolians mentioned who left international careers—in her case as a consultant for Ernst & Young in New York—to go home and work for a better Mongolia. She took a government job and worked closely with Oyun-Erdene on Vision 2050 but soon left her role, as she felt her talents could be put to better use in the tech sector.

"We aim to set up a Silicon Valley tech unicorn, based out of Mongolia, that could be the first mover among Mongolian companies to expand in the global tech market," she tells me. "We will create a hybrid office between Mongolia and the Bay Area, both to access an 'American mindset' but also to empower Mongolians who are part of the brain drain from Mongolia, to become part of this. They can work and live both there and here, the US and Mongolia, and still be compensated at a globally competitive level."

She adds: "There are similarities in the American and Mongolian mindsets. We are both hungry, striving to build something. Many Mongolians want to prove to ourselves that we are global citizens, and for that reason I think Silicon Valley will be incredible for us."

Just as we go our separate ways after lunch, she mentions the statue of Chinggis Khan outside the Government Palace, explaining that her father was the sculptor. "I want to do the same thing," she says, "but in tech." It's hard not to be moved by that level of ambition.

The group's boldest leap of imagination and ambition lies not in its expansion into the US, or indeed anywhere else in the world, however—but into space. Another new company under the ONDO umbrella, ONDO Space, is developing low-bandwidth, bidirectional satellites which, the company claims on its website, will allow customers to communicate from any location on Earth, regardless of blind spots in traditional cellular coverage, helping to unlock the potential of remotely operated IoT technologies, not least for industrial purposes.

At time of writing, the first two satellites were slated to launch in autumn 2023. More fundraising will follow, and, Chinbaatar adds, possibly a flotation of ONDO on the Hong Kong stock exchange down the line. He aims to have 176 satellites, each no bigger than a brick, in orbit within three years. He explains that the company's business model and technology can be compared to those of Swarm Technologies, which was founded by former Google and Apple engineers and is today owned by Elon Musk's SpaceX. Chinbaatar explains that ONDO Space isn't a competitor to companies like Starlink or One Web; its purpose is not to provide broadband satellite internet but rather to enable machine-to-machine communication. ONDO Space has a research and development collaboration with Japan's Kyushu Institute of Technology and has made headlines in Japanese business media.

And beyond launching satellites, Chinbaatar's next high-flying ambition is perhaps even cooler: he wants to use burned-out cube satellites from the ONDO constellation as tiles to build a commercial hotel. Yes, in space. As space tourism fast becomes a real prospect, a growing number of companies and innovators are talking about ventures of this kind, so why not one from Mongolia? Without going too much into technical details, the idea is partly premised on new research by the MIT Media Lab in relation to modular tiles that can autonomously assemble to create habitats in space. Chinbaatar says the space hotel "is something we're working towards" but that it will take up to two decades to come to fruition.

"I have no doubt that ONDO will become a unicorn . . . In fact, I'm very comfortable that we can build a 'decacorn,'" he adds, referring to the term for a company valued at more than $10 billion.

Next time Anar meets foreign investors, perhaps they should wonder not whether he rode in on a horse or lives in a tent but whether he flew in from his space hotel on a rocket.

From the steppe to the world

Another intriguing example of an enterprise taking Mongolian tech and innovation out to the wider world is Steppe Group, a collection of tech development, consultancy, blockchain, and wealth management companies. It was founded in New York, the CEO is based in Hawaii, most of its staff are in Ulaanbaatar, and it has entities in Mongolia, the US, Singapore, and South Korea. Its websites proclaim the company brings "the steppe to the world," and that "innovation thrives in combining disparate ideas and cultures."

Gerelmaa Batchuluun, the group's founder and CEO, says her aim is to "apply nomadic thinking and mentality" to the global arena of tech and finance, an approach she insists enables it to connect companies and investors from both the West and the East.

"For me, the steppe is a place where all can seem very clear and predictable, almost monotone," she tells me in an interview via LinkedIn from her home in Hawaii. "But the reality is quite the opposite. If you are to survive in the steppe, you need to be resilient, steadfast, and prudent. These are values I wanted to engrave into my company."

She adds: "We should always be open-minded and embrace changes and not be left behind when it comes to socioeconomic and tech developments. But at the same time, we need to embrace our own culture, mentality, and heritage."

She started the first company in the group, an innovation and design consulting agency called Steppe Tech, in 2015, with the aim of helping Asian start-ups enter the US market. But she was soon also approached by finance industry clients from Mongolia, who sought help with their digital banking strategies, as well as by Mongolian high-net-worth individuals looking for investment opportunities in American start-ups, real estate, and other sectors. At the same time, she realized that something was brewing in Mongolia, as the country's first wave of home-grown fintech companies began appearing.

"I left Mongolia to study when I was 19," she says. "I always studied and worked abroad and only went home for vacations and to see my family. But when I went back in 2017, it was the first time I saw Mongolia as a potential market opportunity rather than just home. People were hungry for new opportunities."

A year later, Gerelmaa Batchuluun started the Mongolian Fintech Association, a non-profit, and organized the first Frontier Fintech Summit. Emerging as a new face of fintech, she also initiated talks with the Central Bank of Mongolia, the country's Financial Regulatory Commission, its Ministry of Finance, its Committee of Digital Policy, and other bodies, to seek a way forward for the sector. One result of these talks was the establishment of "regulatory sandboxes" designed to protect the financial system from risks while giving rein to innovation. The watchdog agencies also passed a law to regulate the granting of permissions to provide virtual asset services.

As part of the group's expansion, in 2021 she also co-founded a wealth tech firm called ORDA, which allows people to "invest like the top 1%," a reference to the world's superrich. By offering so-called fractional shares in alternative assets, retail investors can use ORDA to speculate in real estate, collectibles, art, commodities, private equity, and other such classes. According to its website, the company deploys a "behavioral finance-based recommendation algorithm" that uses machine learning and data analytics to recommend personalized assets that are tailored to each user's risk profile, goals, and investment style.

Gerelmaa Batchuluun says ORDA is the group's flagship product. She calls it a pathway between emerging and developed markets and proof that "a successful fintech start-up can be built from Mongolia and go global."

When it comes to the future of Mongolia as a fintech and cryptocurrency hub, she believes the country has a lot going for it—but also a number of things that will have to be fixed.

"We like to think of Mongolia as the 'democracy oasis' in central Asia, and we have a young population that's pretty much growing up to be digital native," she says. "I personally believe that there are great preset conditions for the development of fintech here. The population is small in numbers, yes, but it's good enough to gain traction. Mongolia can be used as a launchpad to the global market."

She adds: "If we do it right and well, I believe Mongolia could be a truly unique market and a wonderful place to attract global fintechs. But of course, there is so much groundwork to be done."

According to its PR collateral, Steppe Group strives not only to "reduce inefficiencies in capital markets and bring greater opportunities and returns to investors, but also to find ways of sharing wealth within the community and helping to develop sustainable, healthy economies in frontier markets."

"After a series of tests, experiments, successes, and failures to offer interesting and innovative products and services to our clients, we questioned ourselves," Gerelmaa Batchuluun explains. "Are we just another investment fintech company, or what? Why are we existing? What's meaningful for us to continue on this path? The answer was ESG [environment, social and governance]."

She adds: "Our goal is to make financial markets more democratized and inclusive, yet we understand that there are pressing matters in the world such as climate change, deforestation, social issues regarding gender and education, and so on. Thus, we will only invest where there is an impact on these. That was our pivoting point."

But Gerelmaa Batchuluun isn't alone among entrepreneurs in Mongolia in trying to use technology and innovation to fix social and environmental problems in the country.

Another pair of companies adopting a creative approach to such matters takes Gerelmaa Batchuluun's philosophy about nomadism a step further by referring to it by name. Nomadic PowerBox and Nomadic Cloud are the brainchildren of Chuluuntsetseg "Chuka" Chuluunbaatar and her husband, Tserendorj Natsagdorj, both of whom gravitated to tech from finance backgrounds.

I meet the couple at an SDG Open Day, an outdoor public event in Ulaanbaatar aimed at engaging people with the so-called sustainable development goals adopted by the UN as a universal call to action to end poverty, protect the planet, and ensure that people everywhere can enjoy peace and prosperity. While other exhibitors scramble around, trying to connect to on-site power supplies, Chuka and Tserendorj have no such worries: their exhibit is effectively a power plant on wheels.

Mongolia's "power couple" has built a mobile renewable plant in the form of a van that generates a combination of solar and wind power that can be stored in a battery or plugged into the grid. And on closer inspection, it gets even more intriguing: inside the van, and powered by its energy systems, a computer rig mines crypto. The van is a literal encapsulation of the firm's two arms: renewables (Nomadic PowerBox) and blockchain (Nomadic Cloud).

Tserendorj explains that the van, still at the prototype stage, can be produced at scale and exported to wherever there is demand for renewable energy. Basically, you park the van anywhere, rig up the wind turbine and solar panels, and you're all set. "It's just plug and play," Tserendorj says. "It takes less than an hour to set everything up. Our ambition is that it will be even quicker than that, ideally less than 15 minutes. That's crucial in an emergency situation when you need electricity fast, for example."

For the world's nations and corporations to reach their Net-Zero Emissions goals by 2050, massive amounts of money are going to have to be invested, and Chuka and Tserendorj, along with their third cofounder, Tselmeg Enkhbayar, believe there's room in the global marketplace for innovative power generators such as Nomadic PowerBox.

Low-hanging market segments include organizations that are first responders in disaster areas, and military units that need to set up operations quickly in remote areas. The firm is confident that it can replace diesel generators in power production. And since the van's battery stores the energy it produces, it also has the potential to provide cold storage for the transportation of food or medicines over long journeys. "Mongolia is a testing ground for us," adds Tserendorj. "The big market potential is abroad."

In 2020, Nomadic PowerBox was the winner of Greenpreneur, a global start-up competition organized by The Global Green Growth Institute. Meanwhile, Nomadic Cloud, the blockchain, crypto mining, and datacenter arm of the business, also shows promise. Due to its cold weather, cheap energy, and vast renewable potential in renewable sources, Mongolia has emerged as an interesting hub for data storage and crypto mining, according to several reports.

Chuka explains that she was pregnant with the couple's second child when they first began mining Ethereum—in their own apartment. She shows me photos of machines, cables, and cooling fans all over the place, even on the walls of the washroom. It all looks quite spectacular—and quite dangerous.

"Many small tech businesses started in a garage, right? Ours started in the bathroom," Chuka recalls, as she and her husband fall about laughing at the memory. "I was pregnant, and we had all this equipment delivered to our apartment, and we made a lot of mistakes in the beginning. We're not engineers, and we learned a lot from YouTube videos and different forums. Today, our washroom looks normal again."

When I visited the company's office in downtown Ulaanbaatar in early September 2022, its shelves were stacked full of crypto mining equipment that hummed and growled as it churned through endless virtual currency transactions, generating revenues for Nomadic Cloud in the process.

In the autumn of 2022, however, just weeks after my visit, a software update for the second-biggest cryptocurrency in effect killed the business of Ethereum mining stone dead. The update—dubbed "the Merge"—meant Ethereum miners were no longer required to secure the network, making rig operators redundant.

Crypto is a volatile business, no question. Three or four years ago, virtual currencies had Mongolia buzzing, some international business media identifying the country as the next big regional crypto hub. And the buzz soon went into overdrive, some Mongolians plowing all their savings into digital assets they understood little or nothing about. In August 2021, they even broke the internet, as the phrase goes. Within just 30 seconds of its token sale launching, Inflation Hedging Coin (IHC), a virtual coin created by tech-savvy Mongolian entrepreneurs, pulled in $10 million from thousands of investors, making it one of the fastest-selling assets in crypto history. Since then, many coins issued in Mongolia have been banned under new virtual investor laws, and lawsuits have followed.

For Nomadic Cloud, meanwhile, "the Merge" spelled the end of its mining operation and left it with the headache of deciding what to do with 1,000 or so mining machines. In true entrepreneurial spirit, the firm's founders managed to find ways of repurposing the machines—and came up with two lucrative new lines of business in the process.

One is video rendering, the process by which a computer system methodically processes information from a coded data source to transform that data into something that can be displayed on screens. In other words, rendering converts the source material into the final picture or footage that you can view on Netflix or in movie cinemas, for example. By teaming up with Amazon Web Services' video rendering management system, Deadline, Nomadic Cloud now offers rendering services to companies anywhere in the world.

The second new business line is GPU (graphic processing unit) rentals for AI training. Essentially, global companies involved in data analytics and the processing of large amounts of data—including OpenAI and its chatbot ChatGPT—can perform AI training using Nomadic's GPU-based systems, which are powered by a third-party platform called Vast.ai.

Chuka shows me a map of the world on her phone, large and small bubbles indicating activity on the Vast.ai network. In places like northern Sweden, where energy access is stable and the weather is cold, which lowers the cost of cooling machinery, the bubble is a big one. In Mongolia, there's one little dot.

"That's us," she says enthusiastically. "We're putting Mongolia on the map. As we expand our business with global clients, this bubble will get bigger."

For Mongolia to be able to expand its datacenter or blockchain sectors, however, investments in power generation and infrastructure are a must. Chuka and Tserendorj have their power plant van, of course, but they are clear about what's really required on a national scale: investment from government, development banks, and private companies into energy production, and faster internet connectivity.

In doing good for society, meanwhile, Chuka mentions one more PowerBox enticement. Ahead of the popular summer music festival Playtime, outside Ulaanbaatar, the company planned to offer festival goers the chance to take a warm shower . . . powered by the van. Clever marketing of the Nomadic brand, you might say, but also a good way to reassure parents that their youngsters' personal hygiene is being cared for. What more can one ask of a tech start-up for social responsibility?

Nomadic isn't Mongolia's only firm using blockchain and green tech for social empowerment, though. Another leading light of Mongolia's tech sector, Intelmind, incubates and invests in both its own start-ups and independent ones, sometimes through joint ventures. Its stable of almost 20 companies includes the country's leading e-commerce site, Shoppy.mn, the crypto platform Coinhub, and UB Cab, Mongolia's premier taxi-hailing platform, as well as various other business-to-business, software as a service (SaaS), and IoT development firms. It's like a mini Silicon Valley all of its own.

Success did not come easily, though.

Mendbayar Tseveen, Intelmind's CEO and one of its co-founders, tells me in an interview at the group's offices in downtown Ulaanbaatar—in a building shared with AND Global and several other tech tenants—that he and his partners had previously launched different business, all rather unsuccessfully. They were on the brink of giving up and going back to their old day jobs—but decided to give things one last try.

"Together with the team we said, 'OK, let's do it, let's develop our own product. And if it's not successful, let's just go our separate ways,'" he says. "We made that decision."

It's a decision that led to the launch of Shoppy in January 2017. At the time, e-commerce wasn't popular in Mongolia, and many observers doubted the wisdom of the venture. Much of the country's trade was still done on the gray market, often involving fake branded products. But the Intelmind team decided to swim against this current and focus on original brands. The task they set themselves was made all the more difficult by the paucity of online payment options and fintech infrastructure in Mongolia at the time. A large portion of the population also remained "unbanked," especially in rural areas.

"I remember going to the commercial banks, knocking on their doors, and saying, 'Give us an API to make payments,' but they were not ready," recalls Mendbayar, referring to a type of software interface (an application programming interface) that enables e-commerce businesses to seamlessly communicate with one another and manage payments. "Now it's OK, and everybody understands that e-commerce is a big part of commerce. Everybody is paying attention."

Today, with some 2,000 merchants on the platform, close collaboration with banks and fintech providers, and more than a million registered users—a third of the country's entire population—Shoppy is its dominant e-commerce app and dubbed the "Amazon of Mongolia."

Intelmind's next step was to market its Shoppy platform infrastructure to other companies, which it has done through a spin-off called Cody. Many of Mongolia's most famous firms, such as the fashion brand Michel & Amazonka, as well as international brands targeting the Mongolian market, are now hosted on Cody.

More new start-ups, joint ventures, and investment followed, and the group kept growing. Mendbayar insists, however, that his aim is not simply expansion for the sake of expansion. Rather, he wants to find solutions to the problems facing Mongolian society, help the country's economy diversify away from mining dependency, and inspire and empower a new generation of tech entrepreneurs.

"It doesn't really matter if our company will become a unicorn or not; that's not important," he says. "What's most important is that we give inspiration and passion for other people to create something. Today we survive on mining, but the young generation doesn't want to work in that sector. Many want to develop their own products and make something on their own. I hope young people will continue our journey. That's why we need to be here."

He also mentions a number of services and products Intelmind offers that have a clear social purpose. One of these is the creation of Systems Engineering Mongolia, one of the companies Intelmind has invested in, a "smart well" that gives easier access to clean and warm water in the poorest part of Ulaanbaatar, the Ger district. By drawing hot water from these kiosk-like stations, households don't need to burn coal to heat water at home, which in turn helps to clean up the skies over the capital. And this—the fight for clean skies—is what the rest of this chapter is about.

Powering endless reserves of renewable energy

On a cold day in mid-January, the snow thick on the ground and the air clear and crispy, Sükhbaatar Square is filled with the sound of children's laughter as they swoosh down a slide made of ice. Others stop to admire ice sculptures, their hands tucked deep in their pockets, or try to keep balance on the square's ice rink. The scene would be akin to a winter paradise if it wasn't for one small detail. As darkness falls, and the temperature drops further, a thick blanket of toxic smog spreads over the city.

The reason is that many households, especially in the poorer parts of town, don't have access to central heating. Instead, they burn coal and waste—gigantic amounts of both—for heating and cooking. On cold days like this, Ulaanbaatar becomes one of the world's most polluted cities, up to ten times the safe levels of particulate matter 2.5, as defined in the World Health Organization's air quality guidelines. It's like breathing vomit. It's also hard not to feel dismayed by the thought of children having to suffer this evil. Mongolia's air pollution has been termed a "child health crisis" by the UN children's agency, UNICEF.

But there is hope for a cleaner future, not only for the people here in Ulaanbaatar but for all of Mongolia and the entire region. With the right investments and international support, Mongolia has the potential to become one of the world's leading exporters of renewable energy. According to some assessments, wind and hydropower generated from here could provide power to all of Asia, households and industry. Yes, potentially all of Asia.

The country's combined wind and solar power potential is estimated to be equivalent to 2,600 gigawatts of installed capacity, or 5,457 terawatt-hours of clean electricity generation per year. That amount is enough to meet Mongolia's own energy demands and, with the right transmission infrastructure in place, all of Northeast Asia's, according to a report by the ADB.

For his part, Orchlon Enkhtsetseg, one of Mongolia's best-known green energy advocates and founder of the energy tech firm Ureca, which helps private individuals and companies trade carbon credits, believes ADB is too conservative in its assessment. He thinks the potential is significantly greater.

"We have enough renewable resources to power the entire Asian continent, in terms of solar and wind across the Gobi," he tells me in an interview. "It's quite amazing the level of resources that we have for renewables. Mongolia has great potential to position itself as a leader in sustainability and renewable energy on the international stage."

Orchlon was previously CEO of Clean Energy Asia, which built the largest existing wind farms in the Gobi Desert in close collaboration with the Japanese internet conglomerate Softbank. Softbank's ambition is to create a vast electric power system, called the Asia Super Grid, that will connect China, South Korea, Taiwan, Russia, Japan, and Mongolia—and be powered by wind and solar from the Gobi.

The idea of connecting power plants and customers across Asia has been dreamed of for decades, but the dream has been stymied by issues including a lack of government coordination and infrastructure funding. Now, however, backers see the chance to turbocharge the green transition: connecting renewable energy produced in regions with abundant sun, wind, or hydropower resources to cities and industrial hubs where demand is high and rising. Technology to enable long-distance power lines is also rapidly improving, and the race to renewables in the region is well and truly on.

Scientists in China have a separate proposal to build a super-grid that would connect Northeast Asia's major economies and make renewable energy as cheap as coal. And another group, led by the Australian-Singaporean energy company Sun Cable, in collaboration with universities in both places, is touting a project known as the Asia Green Grid Network that would involve laying a web of subsea cables to establish a continental power grid spanning from Japan to India.

As for Mongolia's advantages, they're not hard to grasp. Known as "the land of the eternal blue sky," the country is practically cloudless for more than two-thirds of the year: the sun shines on average 257 days a year. The steppe and the Gobi Desert, meanwhile, are both exceptionally windy. According to numerous reports, tapping into these resources would guarantee the country's energy security, reduce pollution, contribute to global climate commitments, and grow the economy through energy exports.

On the Chinese side of the Gobi, enormous green investments are already being rolled out. Beijing plans to build 450 gigawatts of wind and solar power capacity by 2030—more than twice the total amount of solar and wind capacity currently installed in the US. Greenpeace East Asia's Li Shuo commented: "This is the positive side of the China climate story. People should get used to big numbers."

Big numbers could become a reality in Mongolia, too, though. The promotional agency Invest in Mongolia points to renewable energy as one of the most promising investment options in the country for international investors, saying that Mongolia has a "huge potential to export renewable electricity across Northern Asia." Meanwhile, a report called "The Renewables Readiness Assessment," by the International Renewable Energy Agency (IRENA), states that Mongolia's mostly untapped renewable resources could be used to kick-start a major cross-border power corridor covering Northeast Asia.

"To decarbonize Mongolia's energy sector, the government aims to increase the country's share of renewable energy, especially wind and solar, which hold great potential for Mongolia," writes James Lynch, Director General of ADB's East Asia Department, in a report.

Much of the financing for renewable energy facilities and infrastructure is being put up by the ADB and the other major development banks. ADB, for example, is capitalizing a new battery-based energy storage system in Mongolia—the largest of its type in the world. It believes the project can put decarbonization of the energy sector on track and help unlock the potential of renewables "to bring back blue skies to Mongolia's urban areas."

As the biggest development player in Mongolia, ADB has also financed several other renewable energy and infrastructure projects in the country. I've heard senior macro economists here saying that "If Mongolia were a football team, the ADB would be Nike, its biggest sponsor." The World Bank, the European Bank for Reconstruction and Development (EBRD), the EU, and other international entities have also invested in the country's green transition.

International engineering firms also see potential. The Swedish-Swiss electrification and automation company ABB is already an important supplier to Mongolia's wind and solar operations, including its Tsetsii and Sainshand windfarms, and its Sumber, Darkhan, Gegeen, and Khushigt solar farms. Now, the firm also sees opportunities in connecting modern mining projects with green energy sources. As a company spokesperson tells me by email, global demand for carbon-free and carbon-transparent commodities is motivating customers to use renewables in production to lower emissions, costs, and downtime.

Mongolia's current power generation capacity includes just 7 percent from renewables, but the government has set a target of 30 percent by 2030. The country's Parliament, meanwhile, has adopted broad measures, outlined in its Green Development Policy and a Law on Energy Conservation and Efficiency, aimed at guaranteeing future sustainability. Invest in Mongolia says the new law will ensure energy security and reliability.

Mongolia could be a huge producer and exporter of renewables, but large-scale, long-term financing is needed to make the industry cost-effective. To make the most of the country's green resources, industry experts are calling for more long-term commitments from investors but also better laws to protect domestic and foreign investors. If somebody invests, the person needs to be confident of realizing a profit, he says: the law must guarantee long-term confidence and not be changed back and forth like it has in the past in ways that have been punitive to business. The arrangements connected to Rio Tinto's investment in the Oyu Tolgoi copper mine could be a benchmark for other large projects, according to various observers.

For Ureca's Orchlon Enkhtsetseg, however, there remains the challenge of connecting lofty national goals with the needs of local people. In the past, he says, this has rarely been done well. When he was implementing large-scale wind farm projects as head of Clean Energy Asia, for example, he became increasingly aware that they had little positive impact on nearby communities. Building the farms meant getting permission from local herders, who tended to be cautious about large-scale projects being built on their land, after having witnessed the destruction wrought by mining developments. Furthermore, Orchlon explains, rumors had spread among herders that the wind turbines would "blow away the clouds," meaning less rain and dryer lands. Herders also worried that the turbines would

153

be fenced off, preventing them from grazing their animals in those areas.

"The first thing the herders would ask was, 'If I support you, will I get free electricity?'" Orchlon recalls. "The answer to that was, 'Unfortunately, no.' The second question was 'Will I get access to the electricity?' Again, 'Unfortunately, no; that's not our job. It's the government's job to connect you to the grid.' Then, the herders would be like, 'So what do I need this for?' From there it was downhill."

He adds: "I thought I was doing something really great, something that was beneficial to the country, to the people, and to the world. My biggest frustration with that was people didn't see it that way. It was really difficult to get that buy-in from ordinary people."

Educated in economics at New York University and having spent most of his life living abroad—his mother was a diplomat and the family moved around to different countries and cities—Orchlon is another former member of Mongolia's diaspora who chose to return. Now a father of two small children himself, he says his ambition to find ways of cleaning up Mongolia's skies has grown more personal.

So, how do you get buy-in from ordinary people for climate-friendly development? The key, Orchlon says, isn't just to build more wind farms or solar farms. Rather, it's to create equitable economic empowerment for ordinary people affected by the transition. And this is what his new start-up is all about.

With Ureca, he says, he and his partners can have direct impacts on people's lives—measured in reduced coal burning and increased family incomes. Officially headquartered in Singapore, Ureca is on a mission to empower and mobilize grassroots communities against climate change by providing a universally accessible platform for carbon offsets.

In short, carbon offsetting occurs when a polluting company buys a carbon credit to make up for the greenhouse gas it has emitted. In theory, the money is then used to fund action somewhere in the world that removes the same amount of carbon from the air. In addition to providing a marketplace for carbon offsets as investable assets, Ureca's "digital measurement, reporting, and verification technology" enables small and medium-sized enterprises and even individual households transitioning to clean energy to produce and sell carbon offsets. These offsetters can range from the homeowner with a rooftop solar panel to a company owning a large wind farm. And yes, this can even be done in the poorest households in Ulaanbaatar's so-called Ger district, named for its abundance of traditional *gers* or yurts.

Because of its underprivileged status, the Ger district is often referred to as a slum or shantytown, but in fact it's very different from the dense, overcrowded settlements that are categorized as such elsewhere in the world. The area grew because of migration to the city from rural areas. These migrants, often former herders, needed somewhere to live and so established a sprawling, informal neighborhood on the outskirts of town, which today remains largely unregulated but is not illegal. During warm summer days, the district can almost look picturesque—children and dogs play in makeshift gardens outside small houses and white tents. There are also restaurants, karaoke bars, convenience stores, and small playgrounds, and the streets are generally clean and safe. That said, life in the Ger district is hard, especially in winter. Hundreds of thousands of people live in the area, more moving in each year.

In collaboration with GerHub—a nonprofit organization that works to find solutions to some of the most pressing issues in Ulaanbaatar's poorest areas—Ureca has launched a pilot project to install solar electricity in a handful of households. By cutting out coal, this produces substantial emissions reductions that can have cascading environmental and social benefits. And it can raise income for people through the sale of carbon credits. It's quite ingenious.

The solution combines AI-based technology that verifies renewable energy generation—both solar and wind—through data collected from smart meters and a blockchain system that links carbon credits to specific producers and keeps track of the exchange of those credits on a live marketplace. This clever, cost-effective system will generate credits even for micro-producers—such as the residents of Ulaanbaatar's Ger district.

In fact, anyone can download the firm's app and trade carbon credits. It's not dissimilar to investing in cryptocurrencies—the major difference being that you are supporting the transition to green energy. Investors can choose where they want to invest, or whether they want to buy credits related to wind generation, solar, forestation, wetlands, or whatever. The firm also offers recommended packages of credits, almost like funds, to make it easier for beginners, and there are donation options. The company has launched a beta version of its trading app, also called Ureca, globally.

"I think carbon credits are a much more sound and lucrative investment compared to some cryptocurrencies," says Orchlon. "There are always underlying assets; there are real forests, real wind farms happening, and so on. We want to open this world of investing in carbon credits to ordinary people, to retail investors. People can look out for their own monetary self-interest but at the same time get educated about climate action."

The platform is also a way to limit the power of brokers and intermediaries, the people who often benefit most from the carbon trade by buying and reselling offsets in bulk and earning large margins.

Many investments in carbon credits today are made by hedge funds and large investment banks that buy carbon credits as an investment class.

"We wanted to bring transparency and integrity to the world of carbon offsetting and carbon financing," explains Orchlon. "If used correctly, we can create a more transparent way to channel funds where they are needed the most. But more importantly, through a platform like this, we could get much more powerful buy-in from people at the grassroots level and at the community level, in a way that aligns to their economic incentives."

Furthermore, by simplifying the world of carbon investing for ordinary people and aligning it with their economic interests, Orchlon hopes to sweep away some of the finger-pointing and "shaming" that seems to surround the climate issue.

"We know that we are screwed when the largest advocate, the person we have delegated this whole issue to, is a teenage girl from Scandinavia," he says, referring to the Swedish environmental activist Greta Thunberg. "That's when you know this whole thing is going not in the best direction. We want to onboard ordinary people in a way that's fun, exciting, and aligned to their economic interests. That's better than, I think, scaring them, or whipping them, saying 'If you don't do this, the world is going to come crashing down.'"

Meanwhile, in the Ger district—far from UN conventions and World Economic Forums, where people such as Greta Thunberg clash with world leaders and investment bankers—small investments go a long way in changing people's lives.

Initial baseline assessments suggest that each household that switches from coal to solar will cut its yearly carbon emissions by 10 to 20 tons and reduce its energy costs by up to 70 percent. That means they can earn somewhere between $1,000 and $2,000 per year producing and selling carbon credits, which is about the same as a yearly minimum wage salary.

Down the line, thanks to increased demand from large corporations for carbon offsets, Orchlon believes the price could rise from its current $100 per ton to $500, meaning a family could potentially earn up to $10,000 annually. That would be a life-changing boost for any Ger district household, no doubt about it.

Powering households with green energy has more benefits than monetary value, however. In fact, when I speak with families in the Ger district, the financial rewards from participating in Ureca's pilot program are quite far down the list of advantages they highlight.

On a sunny Sunday in late April, temperatures slightly on the plus side, I'm invited to the home of a family that has made the green transition. In the middle of their traditional *ger*—where you'll normally find an iron stove connected to a chimney—there stands instead a white electric heating element. The indoor climate is warm and welcoming.

A two-year-old girl, Ankhiluun, runs around the tent playing with a little kitten. Her mother, Amarmend Tsendee, observes her daughter with a smile.

"Before, I always worried that she would fall and burn herself on the stove. It's so dangerous, and it happens often in families here. Even adults have such accidents. Now, I don't have to worry. She can't burn herself on this," Amarmend says, putting her hand on the heater to demonstrate.

A TV, playing on mute, is connected to a satellite dish, and on the electric stove a goulash-like stew bubbles away. By the door, two white boxes contain all the controls to the solar panels and battery banks, and there's also a little green box that allows Ureca to monitor everything.

Together with her husband, Bat-Osshikh Togtohk, a carpenter and woodworker, Amarmend has lived here in the Ger district for almost a decade. They also have a six-year-old son, Dulguun. Their ger is on top of a hill, with a view over the whole city. In the distance, one can see the glittering skyscrapers and luxury hotels of downtown Ulaanbaatar.

"Burning coal is also very time-consuming," the mother continues. "We had to get up at five in the morning, sometimes arguing whose turn it was to start the burning. Then you need to keep the stove running all day. It made the room dirty with dust from the coal. Now, life is so much more comfortable."

Time saved by the couple can now be used for better purposes, such as helping their children with their education. The day before my visit, Dulguun has been tested at school on his knowledge of the alphabet, which he proudly recites for me. His parents beam with pride.

"When our friends and neighbors visit us, they say 'Wow, this is so cool, you really live in luxury now.' They also want to join the program and switch to green energy. I believe many here want to do the same."

Bat-Osshikh Togtohk leans in and says: "Coal is poison. If more households switch to renewable energy, the quality of life for the children in Ulaanbaatar will be better."

Even during the coldest days of the winter, temperatures outside reaching minus 40 degrees, their *ger* was warm, they tell me. They also explain that they can save about $40 a month simply by not buying coal and wood, a welcome boost to the household budget even before the carbon credits kick in.

"Even a small additional income would make a great improvement to our lives," Amarmend says.

159

Davaajargal Sambuu, a single mother of three children, says their lives have also changed for the better since installing green power. We meet up at The Ger Innovation Centre, a gathering place for after-school clubs, workshops, and community events run by GerHub. As we chat, some small girls run around in princess outfits emblazoned with the text "Embrace the Magic"—and it seems there is indeed a sort of magic in the place. People of all ages, from children to their grandparents, can come here to learn, play, and relax. Constructed by the Hong Kong-based design group Rural Urban Framework, the building's double walls—timber and polycarbonate—make the interiors both light and comfortably warm, offering yet another example of how innovation can improve living conditions.

"Living in the Ger district can be hard," says Davaajargal, a resident of 22 years. "But it's also about a mindset. If you think it's hard, it will be hard. If you think it's OK to live here, and try to see things from the bright side, it will be OK to live here."

Now, her house powered by solar panels, life has become more than OK. She says she's "super happy" to be part of the pilot project and has the air of having become something of a green energy ambassador for the district.

"It's a big difference," she adds. "Before, I had to get up so early to burn coal. My hands and nails were always dirty, and it's hard to get them clean from the soot. I was also sad for contributing to the pollution. Now I contribute to a better environment. Many of my friends want to join too. I hope we can change the whole Ger district to green energy."

The families connected to Ureca's pilot project have even started a Facebook group where they share stories about climate change and how to take care of their solar panels to make them more efficient. It's a big contrast to the skepticism of the herders in the Gobi, with their conspiracy theories about clouds being blown away by wind turbines. The difference is that the herders were never directly involved in those projects.

Davaajargal's hopes for the district are matched by Orchlon's ambitions. He explains that the company is in talks with a number of multilateral banks to start introducing financing schemes for local households to collateralize their future carbon credit generation. His vision goes far beyond the Ger district, though. The firm's carbon credit scheme could be extended to households anywhere and everywhere.

During our conversation, he repeatedly comes back to Mongolia's potential as an exporter of renewable energy. The economies of China, South Korea, and other nations in the region are likely to grow faster than those of the US and Europe—and so is their demand for renewable energy. Mongolia, he says, has the ability to bridge the gulf between the supply and demand of clean energy in Asia. Buying energy from Mongolia almost means neighboring countries won't have to ramp up their own production capacity.

"By importing cheap renewable energy from Mongolia, Japan, for example, could expand its cities or build new factories instead of building wind farms or solar plants," he has told the magazine *Mongolian Economy*.

"To conclude," he tells me, "Mongolia has both vast resources of renewable energy and neighboring countries that are rapidly growing. However, to turn this into reality, we need to realize our potential as a nation. We must consciously invest in the renewable energy sector. Due to data-driven economies, electrification, and climate change, we will see growing demand for renewable energy in the next decade. We can position ourselves as a clean energy supplier in Asia."

To realize such ambitions—and find solutions to the other crucial challenges affecting individuals and society—innovators and investors who are able to show long-term commitment will be key. If that happens, I would not be surprised to see some of the young girls from Ulaanbaatar's Girls for Coding bootcamp—and others like them—emerge as tomorrow's creators and disruptors, providing tech solutions that reshape lives in Mongolia and beyond.

As the UN's Tapan Mishra said: "You're the future, you're the powerhouse, you're the engine of change."

4

Empowering the great outdoors

> *Digital nomads, organic lifestyle brands, biofuel, and simulations of space exploration: Mongolia's countryside offers more than breathtaking scenery and traditional tourism.*

The door swings open to the nomadic tent in which we've spent the night. A man pops his head inside the room and asks, enthusiastically, "Wanna see gazelle?"

I roll out of bed, grab my boots, and run after Batbayer, our host. He points to a bright green and sun-soaked hillside a short distance away. But there isn't just one Mongolian gazelle. At least a hundred of these medium-sized antelopes are on the move, slowly and gracefully, and seemingly unconcerned by the humans gazing at them. For the local nomads, such scenes are not uncommon. But for this outsider, it's a magical moment.

Then, from the opposite direction, another group of animals comes strolling toward us, equally uninterested in our presence although without the gazelles' effortless grace. It's Batbayer's flock of sheep, baaing and munching on grass as they go. In less than an hour, the gazelles and sheep have moved on to new valleys, beyond our sight.

Batbayer has a cheerful face, but with the deep creases and leathery tan that come from long hours working outdoors, giving him the look of a sailor from an Ernest Hemingway novel. He lives with his wife, Enkhmaa. Together with his brother, they own much of the livestock they look after as they wander the vast, Mongolian landscape.

Out here, there are no other people around. The steppe of the northeastern Khentii province seems to stretch endlessly in all directions, making the world feel bigger but also somehow simpler. It's only now that I feel I truly understand what they mean by the "endless blue sky." The white nomadic *ger* is equipped with a TV, a satellite dish, and some digital devices, and powered with a mix of solar panels and a diesel generator. Parked beside it are a four-wheel drive and a motorbike. Apart from such conveniences, however, the family is entirely at the mercy of nature.

I ask Batbayar if he's worried that the sheep will run off. There are no fences here, just land without boundaries. He smiles, explaining patiently to the naive city boy that the flock roams freely, typically returning in the evening or the following day. This reminds me that he mentioned the previous evening that he and his brother also had horses. Where are they? Pointing in a wonderful everywhere-and-nowhere gesture, he says he hasn't seen them for three months.

"They like to wander around," he says. "It makes them happy. But they always come back, or I'll find them with help from friends."

"Sometimes," he adds, his sunburned face beaming, "there are more of them when they return because they've had foals."

Mongolia is home to one of the world's few remaining truly nomadic cultures. About a fifth of the population are herders, and nomadism is intricately woven into the country's very spirit. Even its modern-day democratic values can be seen as reflecting Mongolia's nomadic traditions—freedom, independence, and pluralism.

This way of living and interacting with animals and the natural environment—and having respect for both—is not easy for an outsider to fully comprehend. Spending time with people who live a truly nomadic life is eye-opening. It's like entering a parallel universe that is barely visible to the untrained eye and that has almost nothing in common with the hectic, urban lives of most of the world's population. On average, only two people live in each square kilometer of Mongolian territory. Given that more than half the population is crammed into the capital, the chances of running into another human being out on the steppe are remote. The US, with all its wild and open spaces, has 36 people per square kilometer. Japan has 330, Hong Kong almost 7,000. What's more, large parts of the steppe have no regular internet connection, liberating life here from the anxiety and stress caused by the intrusions of all-pervasive social media.

The night before, we feasted at the family home on one of the country's unique and tasty dishes, *khorkhog*, or mutton cooked using hot rocks. This came served with pickled cucumber, a variety of berries, and curdled milk, besides more plates of meat, all from the family's own livestock. A bowl of vodka was passed around, and constantly topped up. (I had been told that it's impolite to refuse, and that a bottle must be finished once opened. I did what I could to accommodate local traditions.) Some neighbors and other family members joined us from their encampments an hour or two's drive away, and we sat jammed up in beds or on small stools around the central stove, listening as Batbayar told stories.

After we drained the vodka, Batbayar magically fished out a bottle of Jack Daniel's, and the atmosphere grew even more jolly. At midnight—to my great surprise—our hosts fired up a karaoke machine and we were soon all dancing to Kazakhstani pop hits and Mongolian love songs, played at full blast under the full moon. The dogs barked, sheep baaed, and millions of stars looked down on us from the infinite depths of the ink-black sky.

As I lay in my sleeping bag later that night, I thought about what I had experienced and how far away we seemed to be from "normal" civilization. How quickly calm settles around us when we're not bombarded by news flashes and text messages. It made me contemplate how mobile phones, and the social pressure to be "liked" and seen online, have elbowed out our basic but more meaningful satisfactions, such as having an uninterrupted conversation, or watching a sunset without feeling the need to post it on Instagram. On the Mongolian steppe, life suddenly felt easier—at least from this perspective.

To a tourist on a short visit, being offline feels like a blessing. But for the nomads who live here, digitalization is fast becoming an important factor in their lives, allowing them to stay connected to friends and family and to conduct business more efficiently.

Anyone who has spent more than five minutes on LinkedIn will surely have encountered someone calling themselves a "digital nomad," a description that refers to the concept of people who feel empowered by technology to break free of the constraints of physical workplaces and roam wherever they please. Picture a tanned Zoomer with a laptop at a beach house in Bali or Goa, most likely earning a living by coding, selling stuff online, trading crypto, or writing.

But in Mongolia, there are *real* digital nomads. In many parts of the countryside, Mongolia's nomads are adapting to modernity— and the technology that underpins it—in their own unique ways, without sacrificing the best of their traditional way of life.

Livestock-based agriculture has traditionally been a backbone of Mongolia's economy and society. However, the country's nomadic way of life has come to be menaced by shifts in temperature and weather patterns, as well as neglect and bad management. Climate change is a major culprit, and Mongolia is already suffering more than most parts of the world. Average temperatures increased by 2 degrees Celsius between 1940 and 2015, while rainfall has declined, leading to chronic droughts and secondary impacts such as dust storms, according to a 2021 report by the World Bank and the Asian Development Bank. This puts the nation's unique ecosystem under pressure.

"Here on the central Asian steppe, the ancient home of Chinggis Khan and his Mongol horde, the nomads are brought up tough," the *Washington Post* wrote in 2018. "Yet their ancient lifestyle is under threat as never before. Global climate change, combined with local environment mismanagement, government neglect and the lure of the modern world, has created a toxic cocktail. The nomadic culture is the essence of what it is to be a Mongolian, but this is a country in dramatic and sudden transition: from a Soviet-style one-party state and command economy to a chaotic democracy and free-market economy, and from an entirely nomadic culture to a modern, urban lifestyle."

Digitalization offers one vital step forward in saving the nomadic tradition. According to Statista, only 12 percent of Mongolia's population was connected to the internet in 2011, but by 2021 this had risen to almost 85 percent. The government sees telecoms and broadband internet as fundamental to improving standards of living in the countryside—through boosting productivity, sustainability, and resilience—and to supporting a fast-growing tourism industry. But it's not just a case of providing connectivity: electronic government services and a digital literacy program targeting herders are also being rolled out nationwide.

As Bolor-Erdene Battsengel, the former vice minister at the Ministry of Digital Development who we met in Chapter 3, states: the new inequality is digital exclusion.

As we also learned in Chapter 3, the sight of herders on horses or camels accessing web services via their smartphones is no longer as incongruous as it might sound. "The e-Mongolia app has made my life easier," a herder named Taivansaikhan tells me when we meet in the wilderness of Khentii province, hours from the nearest village. "I no longer need to go to a government office for different services; I can do it from here. In the beginning, my children helped show me how to use the app, but I'm learning, and I want to learn more."

He adds that the internet connection is still a bit patchy: he sometimes has to drive his motorcycle up a hill to get a better signal and will do all his online tasks while he's up there. But as long as he can make calls to communicate with other herders in the area, he's not too worried.

Many of the livestock here—especially the more valuable breeds such as horses, camels, and cattle—are now implanted with microchips that can be monitored via satellite-based services offered by companies such as ONDO Space. Herders are also increasingly using drones. According to a 2019 paper published by Japanese and Mongolian researchers, these can be used to scan soil conditions, monitor the health of crops, estimate yields, assist in planning irrigation schedules, apply fertilizers, and provide valuable data on weather.

Despite the rapid pace of digitalization, however, traditional herding and nomadic values prevail. During my stay with the herders in Khentii province, it slowly became clear that being online—and tuning into the modern, fast-paced world in general—was not their main priority.

"I would like to use the internet more because it's fun and useful, but the animals like it here; this is a good place for them," Batbayar said when I asked if better internet connectivity would be a decisive factor in his choice of where next to move his livestock. "I would never choose Facebook over the well-being of the animals."

Obvious, when you think about it—or at least it should be.

In the Gobi Desert, another herder, named Khash-Erdene, explains how he balances the online and offline bits of his life. He's part of a new wave of herders who don't live permanently in a *ger* out in the countryside. Instead, he lives in a small village, Khanbogd, and has relatives and hired workers who look after the animals while he manages and monitors things via digital devices. He calls himself a "mobile herder."

"I'm on the mobile or tablet with them, and they show me the animals and the surroundings on the screen," he says. "It's like I'm there with them. I can see the weather conditions, and I can tell them what to do and where to take the animals. I normally read the weather with my eyes, but I'm using different weather forecasting apps to double-check my observations. It's quite efficient."

The mobile herding setup frees up time for him to take on other jobs to supplement the household income, such as working as a driver. This kind of work is plentiful thanks to Khanbogd's proximity to the Oyu Tolgoi mining site. He and his wife haven't entirely abandoned the nomadic life, though: on weekends, they leave the village and head out to the countryside to stay in their *ger*. That's his *real* life, he says.

Still, convincing his children to follow in his footsteps as a herder won't be easy, he says, even as operations become more technologically enhanced and financially rewarding. "Times change, generations change. They help me with the livestock, sure, but they want to go their own way."

Lowering his gaze, he adds: "The herder tradition in our family ends with me."

While many of the younger generation are turning their backs on the hard life associated with traditional agriculture, however, new doors are opening in the countryside. The huge underutilized potential of Mongolia's vast landscapes and of its millions of yaks, camels, goats, and other animals is becoming the engine for an expanding array of new businesses. For example, fashion, jewelry, and cosmetics brands are pushing the country's agricultural sector higher up the value chain and putting the nomad nation on the global map as a source of ecological and environmentally sustainable lifestyle products.

A la mode: Organic cosmetics and fashion from the steppe

When Khulan Davaadorj returned to Mongolia after studying energy and environmental affairs at Columbia University and working for many years in the US and Europe, she realized that she had come back to a different world. The air quality in Ulaanbaatar was much worse than it was when she left, and the extreme climate affected her health in ways she hadn't expected.

She developed eczema, and her skin frequently broke out in rashes. On her doctor's advice, she sought out mild, natural skincare products that would help alleviate the itching without causing further inflammation. There were none to be found on the market locally.

Khulan's solution: she would make her own. That decision led to the creation of the country's first organic skincare brand—Lhamour. Her aim was to not only address her own health issues but to build a local industry that would benefit nomadic herders, farmers, and local manufacturers. Today, Lhamour is the biggest of several Mongolian companies set up to harvest the potential of locally made organic cosmetics. The company's name is a portmanteau of "*Lhamo*" (Khulan's niece) and "*amour*" (the French word for love).

"Our vision is to become an international Mongolian brand that is known for its high-quality and natural handmade products," says Khulan, who left her job at the wind-power firm Clean Energy Asia to set up Lhamour in 2014. "But not only that; we are actually more of a social impact company. That's how I like to consider us."

We meet at Lhamour's headquarters in a charming old neoclassical-style building in downtown Ulaanbaatar. Her office is bright and spacious. On her desk stands an amber-colored rock-salt lamp that she says detoxifies the air.

The company produces more than 70 handmade skincare products, many ingredients of which are locally sourced, as well as other lifestyle products such as bamboo toothbrushes and those rock-salt lamps. It makes soap from yak and goat milk, lip balm, hand creams, nipple creams for breastfeeding mothers, and even a soap made from sheep tails. Khulan has built a unique supply chain of herders and farmers across the country. In terms of distribution, meanwhile, Lhamour's products are widely available in retail outlets in Ulaanbaatar as well as in stores and on e-commerce sites in Japan, Hong Kong, and the US, including the all-organic marketplaces Beautyologie and Pretty Well Beauty. She expects the US will account for around a third of the company's sales within a few years.

The brand has come a long way. Khulan says her years of experience working for big energy companies didn't quite prepare her for the demands of running a startup—and one in an industry she had to learn from scratch. Like many successful startups nowadays, Lhamour was in fact cooked up at home, in the kitchen, to be precise. Khulan used her own food mixers, bowls, and other kitchenware to make her products initially. She got a diploma from Formula Botanica, an organization that runs online courses on organic product development and "indie" beauty entrepreneurship. On top of that, she had to learn all about marketing, design, branding, social media, and of course accounting.

"It was very tough; I was suffering," she recalls. "I was working 24/7. I was working on my birthday. I was working Friday night when my friends were partying. I was working Saturday morning when they were sleeping. It was just because I needed to figure it out. Firstly, it was Mongolia's first organic skincare product, so I had nobody to ask. And secondly, I have no one in my family that has ever done business. It was kind of crazy."

Adding to that early stress, many of her friends and family made it clear they thought she was wasting her time with her little venture, when she could instead be applying her international education and knowledge in banking or mining. "'Why are you doing this?' they would ask. 'You graduated from Columbia University and were working in such huge projects before, and now you're making soaps in your kitchen?'"

But when the company launched its first products, the doubters were quickly won over. "They were actually quite fascinated," Khulan recalls. "Especially the younger people," she adds, laughing. "It was like, 'wow . . . we have our own first Mongolian bath bomb.'" (Having suffered from dry skin all my life, I can testify that her products are pretty magical.)

As alluded to, Lhamour, by elevating previously undervalued ingredients from the Mongolian countryside, is helping to move the country's agricultural sector up the value chain. By exporting to overseas markets, it's also putting those ingredients on the global radar.

"We want to use our traditional Mongolian ancient remedies to produce modern products that work," she told *Forbes* in 2019. "Therefore, we use certain animal fats as well because that is what our ancestors and nomads had been using for years. For example, in the countryside, Mongolian nomads have been using tallow and sheep-tail fat oil for years to help soothe eczema, skin diseases, and rashes, especially for babies and the elderly."

Aware that some consumers in the US and Europe are less inclined to use animal-based products, she believes their hesitation has more to do with concerns over the way animals might be treated. When it comes to Mongolia, such concerns are misplaced, she explained to *Forbes*. "The sheep in Mongolia all live freely in the countryside and are not treated with anything. They eat the freshest grass, and most grasses in Mongolia have medicinal properties as well."

Mongolian sheep actually have considerable pedigree, she added, because they have acclimatized over centuries to frigid winter temperatures.

"They store all their nutrition and vitamins, having the largest tails among all sheep in the world," she told the magazine. "Therefore, Mongolians use the fat from the tail to cook and use on their skin, because it includes natural collagen and all the nutrition needed. Besides sheep-tail fat oil, tallow is also a powerful moisturizer loaded with a wealth of nutrients, essential fatty acids, and antioxidants. It is nourishing and full of lipids that work harmoniously with our skin's oil, called sebum. So we do believe that using these fats is actually even more beneficial to the human skin than some other plant-based oils."

Animal fats are indeed potentially a lucrative business for Mongolia. Beef tallow, lard, and chicken fat are extremely attractive raw materials for biodiesel: according to people I spoke to for this book, the production costs for such fats are substantially lower than for vegetable oils, while the profit margins are higher. Today, much of these fats in Mongolia are wasted, but some people have seen their potential: "The situation is changing rapidly," one entrepreneur who is attempting to build a supply chain for tallow exports told me. "Everyone wants a part of this business now. We can export tallow to all neighboring Asian countries with big margins."

Sea buckthorn, also used by Lhamour, is another interesting commodity. Known for packing in Omega-7 fatty acids, it grows at high altitude and in harsh conditions and has become a popular ingredient in premium beauty care and other products. Mongolia's extreme weather conditions are not a problem for this plant, and people here have been using it in their daily lives since ancient times. What's more, sea buckthorn can be used to encourage reforestation, as its strong, deep, and extensive root system has positive effects on water balance. It's yet another of nature's treasures that could become a money-spinning Mongolian export.

"In Mongolia, we drink sea buckthorn juice all the time," Khulan tells me. "It's a great immune booster."

Sea buckthorn is used to make not only juice but also jellies, jams, teas, oils, fruit wines, syrups, and liquors—and is nowadays increasingly coveted by the cosmetics and pharmaceutical industries. It is believed to help prevent infections, improve eyesight, and slow the aging process. In supermarkets and convenience stores in Mongolia you'll find a wide range of products made from it, and its potential appeal to health-conscious consumers around the world is glaring.

Meanwhile, Khulan's pioneering efforts have not gone unrecognized. In 2015, the Mongolian Chamber of Commerce named her Entrepreneur of the Year, and in 2016, the then-prime minister named her the country's Woman of the Year. In 2021, moreover, Lhamour appeared on "Forbes Asia 100 to Watch," a list of start-ups across the region that are addressing "real-world challenges with fresh thinking and innovative products and services."

Lhamour's success has also prompted the emergence of a host of other Mongolian companies specializing in organic cosmetics.

Battsetseg Chagdgaag, the 35-year-old cofounder of Gilgerem, another organic soap maker, began selling soaps made from camel bone marrow, sea buckthorn, and sheep tails in 2016. In an interview with *Nikkei Asian Review*, she said had been inspired by Lhamour and Goo, another organic skin care company.

"I am proud of [them]; I respect them," she said. "We call them the older sisters, and they are a good example for this industry. They spent their energy and finances to make everyone understand these organic handmade sheep-tail soaps, which paved the way for my business."

Khulan, in the same spirit as her new "sisters" in the industry, tells me that she's "super proud of every single entrepreneur" and everyone who's "trying to make something different" in the country. "It's super important that we support each other," she adds. "I see all these new Mongolian brands as colleagues, even the ones in skin-care. We're in this together."

Commentators say there is no shortage of budding entrepreneurs in Mongolia, suggesting that the initial success of the organic cosmetics industry may draw in more competitors, especially if export sales continue to grow.

"There's really an entrepreneurial spirit here," says Hannes Takacs, country manager for the European Bank for Reconstruction and Development (EBRD). "You can feel the dynamic. Lhamour is such an inspiring story, and it's fantastic what Khulan has built up here."

In 2022, Lhamour was enrolled in a support and funding program run by EBRD called We-Fi, or the Women Entrepreneurs Finance Initiative. Khulan saw it as a way to improve the company's human resource management, allowing her to step back from day-to-day operations and focus more on strategic goals. Before being supported by the bank, she was already engaged in consultancy work for EBRD and conducting baseline studies for female and youth entrepreneurship programs.

EBRD supports projects both large and small but always with a focus on the green and digital economic transition and advancing what it calls equality of opportunity. Over the past 16 years, the bank has supported 132 projects in Mongolia, mostly in the private sector, including several that have helped herders develop business opportunities while reducing their environmental footprints.

"With better management of a herd," Takacs tells me, "a herder can increase their income with less livestock. And of course, it has a positive impact on the environment."

EBRD and other development banks have encouraged Mongolia to process more of its own agricultural output before exporting it. As in the mining industry, most of these resources are currently processed in other countries.

One product with huge potential in this regard is cashmere. Mongolia is the world's second-largest producer of raw cashmere after China, accounting for approximately a fifth of global supply, and the fabric ranks as the country's biggest non-mineral export earner. Cashmere is made from the undercoat of a certain species of goat, and Mongolian cashmere is said to be the best in the world because winters are so cold that these goats develop a particularly dense layer of fur.

While the country has a long history of exporting raw cashmere, however, its value-added processing capacity continues to lag. Today, about 90 percent of the raw cashmere produced in Mongolia is sold to Chinese brokers, according to the Sustainable Fibre Alliance, a non-profit organization concerned with cashmere's environmental impacts. In a 2000 *Wall Street Journal* article, a Columbia University scholar, Morris Rossabi, even called China's hold over Mongolia's cashmere industry—through buying the raw materials and selling back cheap consumer products—"a sort of colonial situation."

Admittedly, much has happened since. And with the right investments, much more can be done to enhance the nation's domestic cashmere capacities. "The cashmere sector in Mongolia has potential to diversify the country's economy, and more sustainable development of the supply chain of the cashmere sector could have a significant transition impact," EBRD has stated in a report. By processing and spinning yarns locally, and by producing its own consumer goods, Mongolia hopes to take one of its primary industries to a new level and establish a name for itself within the fashion industry.

One company that is leading the way in this ambition—and putting the country on the global map for its high-end, affordable, and sustainable fashions—is Gobi Cashmere.

Stroll through its flagship store in downtown Ulaanbaatar on a Saturday afternoon, and you'd be excused for thinking you were in a flashy shopping mall in Singapore or Hong Kong. Tourists from China, Japan, South Korea, Europe, the US, and elsewhere line up at the cashier and changing rooms, while mannequins in chic poses display the latest cashmere trends. With its 2,500 square meters of floor space, Gobi holds the title of "the world's largest cashmere store." This store, however, is just one of dozens of official outlets and franchise stores across the world, from Los Angeles to Tokyo.

The brand has been featured by all of the most illustrious international fashion magazines, *Vogue* stating that wearing Gobi will help to "keep you on trend" and *Elle* recommending Gobi's triangle scarf for "Parisian flare." French magazine *L'Officiel* has referred to Gobi as an "internationally renowned fashion and lifestyle brand," adding that its winter outfits are an "emblem of elegance." Its November 2021 article continued: "Gobi presents a wide range of the ultra-cosy and effortlessly chic styles to buy now and love forever, aiming to disrupt the traditional perception of cashmere."

Amarsaikhan "Ama" Baatarsaikhan, CEO of Gobi's European operations, doesn't hide his pride when I bring up the love-bombing of his company and country by such global fashion bibles.

"We really want to give hope to Mongolian people that a Mongolian company can excel on a global level," he says in an online interview from his office in Berlin. "We want to bring this change. I hope we can be a role model."

He adds: "I see a lot of opportunity to create local brand equity. Like, when you think of cigars, you think of Cuba. When you think of Champagne you think of France. I believe we can create that same equity and build on that; when you think of cashmere, you think of Mongolia."

Gobi Cashmere was founded in 1981 as a state-owned company and was bought in 2007 by one of Mongolia's largest conglomerates, Tavan Bogd Group, which was founded by Amarsaikhan's father, Baatarsaikhan Tsagaach.

The company boasts that its success is not down simply to a combination of fashion, comfort, and quality but also a highly effective supply chain where everything is sourced and made in Mongolia and intermediaries are removed from the equation.

"We have a fully vertically integrated supply chain," Amarsaikhan explains. "We have full control over everything from supplying the raw material from the herders, to cleaning, spinning, knitting, weaving, dying, manufacturing, and the final retail. From a sustainability perspective, we can see exactly how much chemicals, waste, energy, or carbon dioxide emissions we've used or created. We call it 'truly traceable cashmere,' and that's our unique selling point."

Nothing is made in China, he adds, not even the company's machinery or adornments such as buttons and zippers, all of which are sourced from countries such as Japan, Italy, and Germany.

Amarsaikhan says the company has the capacity to make 2.3 million items of clothing a year—or roughly 262 an hour—but at time of writing it was operating at just 50 percent capacity due to the aftereffects of COVID-19. Before the pandemic, in 2019, Gobi reached record sales of around $100 million. Amarsaikhan's dream is to reach $1 billion in sales within 15 years.

Part of this ambition comes from a desire to inspire the next generation. He says he wants to create what he describes as a "monkey effect": if people hear about a company striving for $1 billion in sales, they'll want to copy that aspiration. "I hope people will go, 'Wow, if Gobi could do it, hit the one billion net sales, what can we do to also do that?' It won't be easy—but let's aim high."

Meanwhile, he insists the company's business model is good news for herders and for society in general. Gobi works directly with nomadic herders, producers who, on average, rely on the sale of their raw cashmere to manufacturers for half of their annual income.

"If the cashmere industry is able to succeed, and we create a system that allows herders to be successful, then we will be able to succeed in making sure that our way of life is preserved," Amar-saikhan says.

As more herders are able to make a sustainable living from the countryside, fewer of them will be forced to flock to the Ger district of Ulaanbaatar every winter. In turn, this will have a positive effect on the city's air pollution, congestion, and overcrowding.

Gobi is, of course, far from being the only cashmere player in Mongolia. Visit the State Department Store in downtown Ulaanbaatar, or the airport duty-free area, and you'll be presented with a dozen more brands to choose from, all of them parading similarly ornate and colorful designs. Or, if you're looking for more traditional designs—and considerably lower prices—there's the Narantuul black market.

Post-COVID, Gobi is also reopening factory tours in Ulaanbaatar, where visitors can learn about the garments' production, the cashmere tradition, and about the herding culture and lifestyle. And this leads us seamlessly to the other major industry covered in this chapter—tourism.

Entering the Netflix tourism race

Standing outside a nomad ger, the old man and the boy watch as a group of riders approaches from across the steppe. Even at a distance, it's clear that they're soldiers. They stop in front of the tent, and their leader—his face covered by a dark hood—dismounts and walks toward where the old man is standing. The boy runs inside for a sword.

"I'll protect you father. I'll protect the book," he says, ready to attack.

The old man lays his hand on the boy's arm, giving him a nod to lower the sword.

"The time has come; I was told in a dream last night," he says.

When the soldier takes off his mantle, they see that it's the warrior Boruchu—Chinggis Khan's most loyal ally. The old man invites him into the tent, and they sit down.

"I've heard that you have the secret book. Chinggis Khan has sent me for it," Boruchu says, and the old man—whose family has been guarding the book for generations—takes it from its hiding place and hands it to him.

In the next scene, we see Chinggis Khan reading the book, an account of the empire of the Huns, a nomadic group of horseback warriors who swept out of Central Asia and into Europe between the fourth and sixth centuries.

This is a rough summary of the opening of a planned historical TV drama series from Fantastic Productions, one of Mongolia's leading content creators. As you may have deduced, the series tells the story of the Huns, as viewed through the eyes of Chinggis Khan as he reads the history of his ancestors.

For Fantastic's founders, the project is about more than just creating a thrilling drama with gruesome battles and sizzling love entanglements. It's also an opportunity to portray a more authentic take on Mongolian history.

Fantastic's offices buzz with creative endeavor. Posters from some of the country's most successful films and TV series adorn the walls, alongside storyboards for the new series. Everywhere I look, there are costumes, weaponry, and other props. Even the producers' hair is on point: besides writing and directing the show, they've cast themselves as Hun warriors and have grown their hair long for the purpose. (Being in front of the camera, it should be noted, is no novelty to them: before Fantastic came into being, its founders were already household names as members of the country's hottest boy band, Boom Town.)

"We're trying to capture what's true," says Tamir Bat-ulzii, director of the new series and one of the company's founders.

Like many Mongolians I speak to, the Fantastic team takes the view that foreign-made productions have mostly done a poor job of representing the country's cultural heritage, Netflix's *Marco Polo* being just one high-profile recent example.

"Mongolia's history is being translated differently by different people, and we are afraid that we're losing control of our past," Tamir Bat-ulzii explains.

Beyond a mission to correct the perception of Mongolia's past, he says he and his colleagues want the three-season show—which they aim to finance and distribute via one of the major American streaming platforms—to help redraw the country's current cultural landscape.

"If we set up a production that meets international standards, it will benefit not just us but all filmmakers here," he tells me. "It will make a big change for the whole industry. It could also lead to more international production companies coming here and using Mongolia as a location for filmmaking."

His words echo the ambitions of the Mongolian government. To diversify the country's economy, it aims to develop Mongolia's creative industries and lay the foundations for new sources of growth other than mining.

"Everybody is looking at mineral commodities. But we feel that our culture is another commodity we can offer to the world," says Nomin Chinbat, minister of culture, in an interview at the newly established government department. "Culture is a key sector to diversify our economy, and filmmaking is one of the main areas."

Before taking up her role as minister in 2021, the Harvard Business School graduate was already a well-known face on Mongolia's cultural and hospitality scenes. In 2008, she established the Terelj Hotel & Spa, one of the country's first 5-star hotels. A year later, she launched an independent broadcast firm, Mongol TV, serving as CEO until January 2021.

In recognition of her achievements, Chinbat was selected by *Forbes Mongolia* in its "30 under 30" list of young movers and shakers in 2017, and as one of the "Top 25 Women in Television" by *Hollywood Reporter*. The World Economic Forum has said of her: "Through her professional work in media and her active role in social initiatives she has become one of the opinion shapers and role models for young people in Mongolia."

Given her background, it's no big surprise that the Ministry of Culture looks more like an art gallery than a traditional government office building. Its rooms and corridors are light and welcoming, while the walls are hung with works by local artists that get rotated regularly.

"When I took on the Cabinet job, it was to develop a creative industry but also to promote Mongolia internationally," she says. "I was thinking: 'How do we identify ourselves internationally? What can Mongolia offer to the world? How are we going to be differentiated in the world?'"

One answer, she says, was offered by nomadic culture—and how Mongolians have for centuries lived in harmony with nature. "The philosophy of nomadic culture is the sustainable lifestyle that we have—and it's what the modern world is looking for. Like, 'How can we be more sustainable? How can we be off-grid?' This is a philosophy that's already embedded into our culture. It's part of who we are. So that's one selling point we are building on."

She adds: "It's very different from what other parts of Asia can offer. It's very different from what the West can offer. It's really unique."

Three specific bills have been passed since Chinbat took up her role: one on cultural policy, one on film, and one relating to museums. All three are geared toward boosting Mongolia's cultural sector and building soft power internationally.

The legislation on supporting the film industry, passed in early 2022, created incentives that include reimbursement of some production costs. The immediate aim is to attract global film and TV projects, create jobs, and build capacity; ultimately, it's to build greater awareness of the country's unique heritage among investors and tourists alike.

"We want to make it easier for our film industry to thrive and also try to bring more international filmmakers into Mongolia," Chinbat says. "Promoting filmmaking is a way to promote Mongolia internationally."

According to *Tourism Tattler*, a trade magazine, film-driven tourism is a rapidly growing sector. In other words, when deciding where to go on holiday, people are increasingly influenced by the films or TV series they've watched. Moreover, there's ample evidence to show that proactive policies to entice filmmakers to a given locale will drive subsequent tourist traffic.

There are many examples of this in action. During a trip to Tunisia some years ago, I visited an underground Berber cave dwelling that had been used as the location for Luke Skywalker's boyhood home—the so-called "Lars homestead"—in the Star Wars movies, a spine-tingling experience for any fan of the franchise. Tunisia's southern regions boast 12 Star Wars filming sites, and a tourism official told me that "Star Wars tourism" remains a major draw for international visitors more than 40 years after the original movies were released.

Meanwhile, a 300-percent increase in visits to Scotland in the 12 months following the release of Mel Gibson's 1995 epic *Braveheart* is attributed entirely to the film. Similarly, the Crown Hotel in Amersham, England, whose Courtyard Suite features in *Four Weddings and a Funeral* (1994), was fully booked for three years following that movie's release. And *The Beach* (2000), starring Leonardo DiCaprio, was said to be responsible for a 22 percent increase in young travelers visiting Thailand.

Filmmaking also brings direct income to local economies during shooting. According to the American Motion Picture Association, Marvel's *Black Panther* employed more than 3,100 local workers in the US state of Georgia, who took home more than $26 million in wages, while 20th Century Fox's popular television series *This Is Us* contributed more than $60 million to California's economy during filming.

Perhaps the highest-grossing example of movie tourism outside of Hollywood is New Zealand, where Peter Jackson's *The Lord of the Rings* was largely shot. In the two decades after the first of the films premiered, the number of international visitors to Wellington leapt by 87 percent, according to a 2022 article in *National Geographic*. Tourism New Zealand has found that nearly one in five visitors first discovered the country through *The Lord of the Rings* and Hobbit films, and that a third of all tourists visit a location from the films during their stay. In 2019, "Tolkien Tourism" was worth $420 million to the local economy.

When *Variety* asked Jackson why he chose to shoot the films in his native New Zealand—then better known for its arthouse and indie productions—rather than Hollywood, he quipped: "Why would I leave the Shire to go and live in Mordor?" With its vast steppe lands and nomadic culture, Mongolia could potentially offer similar levels of Middle-earthian tranquility.

In September 2022, Mongolia's Ministry of Culture and National Film Council welcomed representatives from production companies such as Netflix, HBO, Paramount Pictures, and Warner Brothers to help them learn more about the country's film industry and how they can use Mongolia as a location.

"Mongolia has entered the race to attract big-budget global productions," the *Hollywood Reporter* wrote. "The generous nature of the program is certain to make Mongolia a competitive territory in the global race to attract high-profile Hollywood shoots."

The "program" comprises a flurry of incentives launched by the government to spur more TV and film production in the country, but the biggest lure in the package is a 30-percent cash rebate available to productions in Mongolia involving a minimum spend of $500,000.

A similar 30-percent rebate system is also being established for projects that employ a substantial number of Mongolian personnel on postproduction work. And there are two other rebates: a 10-percent incentive available to productions that highlight Mongolian culture and heritage, and a 5-percent incentive for productions that use foreign crew and talent. Significantly, these last three incentives may be combined to generate an overall rebate of 45 percent for projects that tick all the boxes.

Meanwhile, for projects that don't quite meet those criteria, there is still the Mongolia Film Incentive. This dangles a 20-percent rebate in the direction of local or joint-film productions that are deemed to promote Mongolian culture and heritage to international audiences.

"We have been promoting Mongolia as a location since 2017, when we joined the Association of Film Commissioners International," Orgil Makhaan, president of the Mongolian National Film Commission, told *Variety* in 2021. "Now we have a government that is willing and planning for development of the content industries. There is no reason why, over time, Mongolia cannot be the next New Zealand."

Makhaan said that major selling points include Mongolia's connectedness (Ulaanbaatar is a 1.5-hour flight from Beijing, three hours from Seoul, and seven from Berlin); sunshine on 80 percent of days annually, even in winter; four distinct seasons; cityscapes reminiscent of ex-Soviet Bloc architecture; and hugely varied landscapes (notably deserts, icy mountains, steppe-grasslands, and dense forests).

The country has already been put on-screen in shows such as the Netflix-Studio Dragon Korean drama *Crash Landing on You*. One of the most poignant moments in the series is when the main characters, Se-ri and Jeong Hyeok, spend a night under the open sky after their train journey to North Korea's capital, Pyongyang, is delayed. The scenes were shot in Ulaanbaatar, and the Mongolian capital also stands in for Pyongyang when they finally arrive at their destination.

There are in fact quite a number of existing films that might inspire you to travel to Mongolia; for example, *The Story of the Weeping Camel*, *The Cave of the Yellow Dog*, and *The Two Horses of Genghis Khan*. (When you have time, search for "The Story of the Weeping Camel—song" on YouTube, to discover an emotionally charged scene in which a nomad family tries to get a female camel to accept a calf that has lost its mother. A Mongolian friend told me that this scene, perhaps better than any other, explains the connection between nomads and their animals and the close connection Mongolian people feel with nature.)

Another production that is making global waves, not on the big screen but rather on stage, is *The Mongol Khan*. Produced by Hero Entertainment, one of the country's foremost theater companies, the production, with a cast of over 70 played a blockbuster run in Ulaanbaatar in 2022 and was due to hit the London Coliseum in the winter of 2023. After a limited season in the UK, it will travel to New York, Tokyo, Seoul, and possibly other international destinations.

A lavish revival of a 1998 play by Mongolian writer and poet Lkhagvasuren Bavuu, *The Mongol Khan* is billed "as an introduction to the country and its history, giving audiences and would-be travelers a taste of the rich culture of this remarkable nation."

"The Mongolian theater production playing in the West End for the first time is an historic event, and marks a new era in Mongolian drama," Hero Baatar, the founder of the company and director of the play, said in a statement. "Cooperation with British artists is a crucial step in developing Mongolian theater, and it is a great honor for us to work with artists from Shakespeare's homeland."

The production also forms part of the celebrations for the sixtieth anniversary of diplomatic ties between Britain and Mongolia.

I meet Baatar in the production company's studio in downtown Ulaanbaatar, just hours before watching the play later in the evening at the Mongolian State Academic Theatre of Opera and Ballet. The studio is full of sketches, costumes, and props from this and previous productions; there are shelves of books, paintings, and instruments, as well as a small stage and a bar, making the place feel like an explosion of creativity. Baatar explains that his half-brother, Prime Minister Oyun-Erdene Luvsannamsrai, helped a bit with the script, perhaps to "get some rest" from his hectic day job.

The show is a bombastic, large-scale production, for sure. It also has all the ingredients of a classical tragedy: jealousy, mistaken identity, adultery, rivalry, sacrifice, succession, and the struggle for power. Based on historical events, it explores the evolution of Mongolian culture through a gripping 2,000-year-old story, brought to life through a stunning original score, dance, puppetry, and elaborate sets and costumes inspired by traditional nomadic culture. "A brutal succession battle threatens the very heart of the Empire," writes *Theatre Weekly*. "As the great Khan struggles to maintain his supremacy, a plot unfurls that will forever alter the balance of power." (I wouldn't be surprised if *The Mongol Khan* eventually becomes a Netflix series; again, it has all the ingredients of a great drama.)

The Mongolian creators are collaborating with an international team of world-renowned artists and practitioners on the show's development, including the historian and travel writer John Man, an expert in Mongolian history and culture. The entertainment magazine *Time Out* writes that little is known in the UK about the upcoming theatrical play: "But we can be certain of two things: it's Mongolian, and it's spectacular." It is, indeed.

The Silk Road to Mars

If big film crews visiting a country can generate good income, the same can surely be said for visiting astronauts and space exploration teams. We touched on space tourism in the Chapter 3, and now we'll look at another interstellar project taking shape in Mongolia, this time deep in the Gobi Desert.

A group of Mongolians have launched a project called Mars V, aiming to assist in achieving humankind's vision of reaching Mars. Essentially, it entails building a simulation center in one of the most inhospitable places on Earth, where astronauts and scientists can prepare for missions in extreme environments on other worlds, including the Red Planet. Having temperatures ranging from +45 to -45 degrees Celsius, the Gobi is perhaps the ultimate location for such exercises. The prospect of leveraging it as a Mars research laboratory could have enormous scientific, economic, and social value for the country.

Mars V's CEO Erdenebold Sukhbaatar refers to the idea as "Mars on Earth."

"The Mars project is humankind's next giant leap," he tells me in an interview at his office in Ulaanbaatar. "It's our next mission. Many innovators are doing such a great job [for Mars exploration] and I want Mongolia to play a part in this and be part of the future."

He adds: "We want to make great contributions to humankind. We're a small population with a great legacy. We are doers."

The office walls are covered with space-themed posters and paintings, some displaying astronauts and rovers on Mars, as well as photographs of the founding members—all dressed in Mars V sportswear. In a cupboard are spacesuit helmets and other equipment, and bright orange-red blob-shaped lamps add to the intergalactic atmosphere.

Some of the wealthiest people on the planet—including Jeff Bezos, Elon Musk, and Richard Branson—have made huge investments over recent years in visiting, exploring, and colonizing space, and modern space exploration and the global competition to reach Mars has sparked both civil and military innovation in the field. Simulations of Mars on Earth can help to anticipate and allay some of the physical and mental challenges astronauts are likely to face when they do go.

Thanks to projects such as Mars V, a large number of people are expected to travel to Mongolia for training and research activities. Again, this offers a new way of utilizing the Mongolian countryside that can help to diversify the economy away from mining and away from the capital. Already, NASA is seeking applicants to participate as crew members during one-year simulated missions in the US, which will require large numbers of onsite engineers, scientists, and supporting staff.

"Thousands of people will come to Mongolia, not primarily to go to the Chinggis Khan monument or on wilderness adventures but for this special-interest tourism," says Erdenebold.

According to the promotional blurb on the company's website, it aims to launch "a special-interest tourism program that provides individuals the special experience of exploring the Red Planet under a habitat that most closely resembles the Red Planet."

(Across the border in China, the Mars Base 1 Camp in the Gobi—comprising several interconnected modules, including a greenhouse and a mock decompression chamber—has already opened its doors to the public and hopes to attract visitors who want a taste of what it might be like on Mars. "I am very excited to be here," a 13-year-old student from Jinchang told Reuters. "We saw the monolith, a crater, and a cave. It's better than the Mars that I had imagined." Meanwhile, at a Mars site in the Utah desert in the US, reports suggest isolation simulation has been somewhat ruined by tourist numbers and intrusion by trespassing drones. "Drones are banned from flying over private property, and trespassing is illegal, but tourists wander about the station, stare inside the buildings, or just sit on the hills outside the airlock waiting for the 'astronauts' to take their daily

EVA," Screenrant wrote in 2021, referring to "extravehicular activity," or spacewalks. The Mars V team is keen on attracting visitors, but it's hard to imagine there will be similar flocks of trespassing tourists in the depths of the Mongolian Gobi Desert.)

Erdenebold—a Harvard Kennedy School alumnus who also happens to be one of the leaders of the Mongolian Democratic Party—has, together with his colleagues and other supporters, created a lot of attention for the Mars V project around the world. The group has connections with NASA, the European Space Agency ESA, SpaceX, and other organizations. They've had talks with India's President Narendra Modi and former US President Donald Trump. The team has close contact with Alyssa Carson, a NASA astronaut in training who has been officially nominated as the first person the agency hopes to land on Mars. Mars V's board of advisors includes Robert Zubrin, president of the Mars Society and author of *The Case for Space*.

Zubrin has written an essay about his first visit to Mongolia and the Gobi Desert in 2022, observing: "I expected Mars V to be perhaps a dozen local Mars enthusiasts. Instead, it turned out to be a highly influential organization with some *three thousand* members, including corporation and bank presidents, prominent cultural figures, political party leaders, and Mongolian government cabinet members."

The essay goes on to explain the advantages of locating a simulation center in the Gobi desert, how nomadic thinking has been applied in the project by having not just one fixed site but a number of movable structures, like *gers*, and the benefits of Mongolia's neutral diplomatic position.

"The Gobi Desert provides a unique and vast theater of operations to learn about how to explore Mars," Zubrin writes. "This is of critical value, because all the thinking by NASA, other space agencies, and even SpaceX about human Mars missions has been about flight systems, with virtually none devoted to surface activities—which are the entire purpose of the mission. There is no point going to Mars unless you can do something effective when you get there. Situated in free, but non-aligned Mongolia, the Gobi Mars Analog Research Station could provide a place where those seeking to look up from our increasingly fractured world still can come together to learn how to do that."

Zubrin also waxes lyrical about Mongolia's "space nomads" and the country's potential as a major space industry player. "As for the Mongols themselves," he states, "I think they will play a significant role not only in their own desert station program but in the human Mars missions that follow. I think there will be Mongolian astronauts among the crews that go to Mars in the near future. And someday, I think there will be Mongolian starship captains."

Such a project might epitomize the wild dreams of overoptimistic entrepreneurs, sure. But Erdenebold has little doubt that Mars V will bring significant benefits to Mongolia, allowing it to enjoy a slice of the multitrillion-dollar space market as an independent player. "If our project is good enough, SpaceX and other organizations will financially support us and come to Mongolia," he says. "We're talking about millions of dollars, maybe billions."

Chinggis Khan and community tourism

Due to its incredible landscapes, rich history, and fascinating nomadic culture, Mongolia offers a truly one-of-a-kind adventure, many and varied avenues opening toward an economy that is diversified away from mining. From backpackers to bankers, everyone seems to agree on that.

Just sample the introduction from Lonely Planet's latest guidebook: "Mongolians are fully aware of the unique beauty of their country. Ask locals and they will probably start gushing about the spectacular countryside, vast steppes, rugged mountains, clear lakes and abundant wildlife and livestock. Some areas are so remote you could drive a full day and see almost no signs of human habitation. It's this true wilderness experience that many people find so appealing, and city residents from Ulaanbaatar frequently hit the road to camp. Protected areas cover almost a fifth of the country and the government is looking to increase that figure."

The World Bank, meanwhile, describes the nation's potential as follows: "Mongolia has a unique value proposition from a tourism endowment perspective, with strong niche products for leisure tourism linked to the country's diverse nature and stunning sceneries; the nomadic lifestyle and Mongolian culture and festivals; the historical legacy of Chinggis Khan; and sports and adventure tourism that thrive during a relatively short tourism season mainly between May and September."

In 2019, some 637,000 tourists visited Mongolia—a record high and up by a third compared to the number five years earlier. Tourism revenue that year reached $605 million, almost three times higher than it was a decade earlier and, World Bank data show, accounted for 7.2 percent of GDP and 7.6 percent of total employment.

Then came the COVID-19 pandemic, and tourism shuddered to a stop.

Travelers are now returning to Mongolia. At time of writing, some disruptions were still being felt, according to people I spoke to, from the pandemic hangover, the war in Ukraine, and generally slowing global demand. But industry insiders are confident numbers are on an upward trajectory.

"The government is doing a lot to support the sector now, including more direct flights and making it easier for people to get visas," Dirk Bansemer, general manager of the Kempinski Hotel in Ulaanbaatar, one of the capital's most established international hotels, tells me. "Business travel is back to normal; that recovered fast, at least for us. The Oyu Tolgoi mine has a positive impact on this segment."

The government has introduced various policies and initiatives aimed at promoting the sector. These include developing new tourism infrastructure, such as hotels, airports, and roads, as well as establishing national parks and protected areas to preserve Mongolia's unique landscapes and ecosystems. Still, much more needs to be done to create a level of tourism infrastructure that meets the needs of international travelers. That is perhaps especially true when you consider that visitors to Mongolia are often looking for outdoor adventures in the wilderness rather than an easy leisure getaway.

Hours spent driving in jeeps or vans over the rough terrain of the steppe, often with no real roads, isn't all that appealing to those with bad backs or sensitive bottoms, and I could see dread in the eyes of my friends from Singapore—more used to air-conditioned shopping malls than outdoor escapades—when I told them there are no washrooms when you stay with the nomads.

There are of course exceptions, such as Nomin Chinbat's Terelj Hotel & Spa, nestled in one of the most carefully protected areas of the country, Gorkhi-Terelj National Park, and just a short drive from the capital. Or the newly opened Yeruu Lodge, run by Veronica Beijer from Sweden and Eirik Gulsrud Johnsen from Norway, which offers a comfortable yet adventure-laden taste of the countryside—including activities such as horse riding, kayaking, yoga, and meditation—and is just a few hours' drive from Ulaanbaatar.

Still, the lack of resources allocated to infrastructure development, and Mongolia's protectionist aviation policy, have impeded the sector's development, according to a World Bank enterprise survey of tourism companies in early 2021. Other reports also state that the government's goals for the tourist sector are overoptimistic and don't correlate with infrastructure facilities or hotel capacity on the ground.

That said, the Vision 2050 roadmap does unleash several investments and initiatives over the coming years, which will go a long way toward modernizing the tourist sector and its supporting infrastructure. (The section of the roadmap on tourism in fact falls under a broader chapter on infrastructure and sustainable agriculture, which makes a certain sense.)

In Khentii province, for example, large-scale investments are now being made in collaboration with international development banks, especially ADB, to spur "economically inclusive" tourism and conservation—and to support "Chinggis Khan tourism."

One late September afternoon, I stood on a small hill facing the setting sun. I closed my eyes and stretched my arms out as wide as I could. On instructions from my guide, I asked the spirit of Chinggis Khan to give me and my family strength and wellbeing. Before this ritual, we had also asked for the great emperor's guidance while walking three laps around a monument at the Deluun Boldog Hill, a messy-looking thing made of rocks, sticks, and textiles. Some visitors knelt in quiet prayer in front of the monument. Yes: here, at what is believed to be the birthplace of the first great Khan, he is considered to be almost a God.

"We want to invite everybody to learn more about Chinggis Khan and our history, as well as experience the beauty of nature," a local politician told me. "We also want Mongolians from all over the world to feel welcomed back to experience the birthplace of Chinggis Khan and reconnect to their roots."

There's also a fear among some people here—including the government—that new Chinggis Khan complexes and initiatives in China and Kazakhstan are trying to "steal" the heritage of the Khan empire from Mongolia.

It's quite amusing—when you stand there in this magnificent region of lakes, rivers, and forests—to imagine how the greatest warrior of all time must have run around these woods and hills as a kid. The day before, I had been taken to the Friendship Monument, a magnificent statue of Chinggis Khan shaking hands with Boruch. It's a place where good friends or young lovers go to attest their bonds to each other—the two great warriors as witnesses. There are in fact several such Khan-related sites in the area. There are also many weeklong tours on offer to experience the region and to discover "the beauty of Eastern Mongolia, its wilderness, and many historic sites connected to Chinggis Khan's childhood, his battles, his loves, as well as his offspring," as one tour operator puts it.

Now, Khentii province is gearing up to welcome a surge in Chinggis Khan tourists. A multimillion-dollar Chinggis Khan Tourism Complex is being built, along with supporting roads, parking lots, waste-management facilities, and other examples of vital infrastructure. The complex will be in the Onon-Balj National Park, where the Mongol helmsman grew up, and is being funded by a $38 million loan from ADB to develop ecotourism, part of which will also go to the Khuvsgul Lake National Park, Mongolia's largest freshwater resource.

The loan, which was announced in 2019, marks ADB's first disbursement in Mongolia specifically focused on tourism and the management of protected areas. The projects, the bank says, will benefit around 11,000 residents, as well as aiding local conservation and climate change adaptation and mitigation efforts.

"Tourism is the largest and fastest-growing sector of the global economy, and Mongolia's magnificent landscapes and unique heritage can capitalize on this," said ADB Senior Environment Specialist for East Asia Mark Bezuijen in a press statement. "That said, ADB's support will help ensure that tourism growth in Mongolia benefits local residents and preserves fragile environments over the long term."

According to the bank, the emphasis is on community-based tourism that supports visitors and generates local income. Besides upgrades to infrastructure, the funding will be used to improve management of wilderness areas. The projects also align with Mongolia's National Program on Tourism Development, 2016–2030, and the government's efforts to diversify the economy, build climate-resilient infrastructure, protect the environment, and increase economic opportunities for residents in rural areas.

By 2028, ADB forecasts that tourism will provide 149,000 jobs and $2.1 billion in revenue, accounting for 11 percent of Mongolia's GDP.

But it's not only projects with big budgets attached that will make the difference. There are many interesting, although less large-scale, sustainable, and community-based tourism initiatives in Mongolia. I'll mention just a few.

The Gobi Oasis Tree Planting Project aims to combat desertification in the Gobi Desert through the planting of thousands of trees. Ger to Ger is a community-based tourism organization that connects travelers with nomadic families, offering authentic cultural experiences while promoting sustainable and responsible tourism. The Three Camel Lodge is an eco-friendly luxury getaway in the Gobi Desert that emphasizes sustainability, cultural preservation, and community development. These examples demonstrate that sustainable tourism initiatives in Mongolia not only contribute to environmental and cultural preservation but also create economic opportunities, while raising awareness about the country's unique heritage and natural resources.

New life for an old mine

This book started in the mining town of Berkh, where some of our main protagonists grew up, and we'll end it there too. As mentioned in the introduction, the town highlights how mining can bring wealth and prosperity to a region—but also how quickly this can turn to despair when the deposits run out and not enough money or efforts have been invested in other sectors.

Now, after decades of slumber, the old fluorspar mine in Berkh is being brought back to life. And so, hopefully, is the local economy.

During a visit to the town in September 2022, I was invited to visit the site of the mine, which is now being turned into a museum, more than 50 meters below ground. Wearing hardhats, headlamps, and warm jackets, we squeezed into the mine's old lift, which squeaked and rattled as it took us down the shaft. An engineer assured us it was all safe.

Down there, it's cold and damp. The snaggy, cavernous tunnel stretches in both directions, lit by LED string lights. Water drips from the ceiling, creating small puddles. In the dim light, stone statues of mine workers look like real people approaching from the depths of the darkness.

For all the obvious reasons, it's hard not to think about the tunnels collapsing, or what would happen if the lights suddenly went out, or if we couldn't find our way back through the warren-like passages, or . . . the imagination starts spinning. This is a high-adrenaline museum; no doubt about it.

Naturally, safety is the priority for the museum's engineers—just as it was when the mine was active—something we're repeatedly reminded of.

Walking along seemingly endless tunnels brings us face to face with the working conditions these miners endured and the harsh realities of mining through the centuries. Monuments and machinery along the walls provide a record of the industry's evolution: from its reliance on horses and human muscle to more modern technology. Being down in a real pit makes it easy to grasp how hard it must have been for workers toiling away deep underground, breathing toxic fluorite dust, their lives on the line if anything went wrong. At the same time, it's also a chance to appreciate the huge technological advances the industry has made in automation and safety. In the most advanced mining operations, internet-connected remotely controlled robotic equipment and vehicles have removed or limited the dirtiest and most dangerous work.

Our tour is led by Enkh Javkhlan, the governor of Berkh, and we're accompanied by several mine workers to make sure we're safe. At the time of publication, the site was still being renovated.

"When the mining museum is open, we will have many people coming here," the governor tells me. "This will blow new life into our community. We'll also benefit from the many other tourist attractions that are being established in the region, including the Chinggis Khan tourist project."

When it opens, the museum—officially called the Mongolian Underground Mining Museum, Research and Training Center—will have cafés, music and entertainment halls, conference rooms, and souvenir shops, as well as exhibition rooms sponsored by Rio Tinto and other international mining players. Why not also hotel rooms, one might ask.

The ground-level compressor building will house those parts of the museum that aren't deep underground. Meanwhile, the education center will be based in the mine's second shaft and its administration building—and will be a vital facility for students majoring in mining and mineral engineering.

Enkh Javkhlan explains that students from local and international mining universities are expected to stay weeks or even months at the site, to experience what things used to be like and learn about modern mining technologies.

He adds that the winds of change are already being felt in the town. New, modern residential apartments are under construction, and a local school has signed an affiliation agreement with a British university. A local poultry factory, specializing in a particular type of smaller egg that's regarded as a delicacy, is also investing to increase production for exports. People are slowly moving back.

During the weekends, residents are even going dancing at the Cultural Center—just like during the boom years. At the center's entrance stands a large Soviet-style sculpture of the old mine, made of fluorspar: a reminder of the old days. Snatches of hip-hop and electronic beats, played by local youngsters after school, tell a different story—of a new era.

"I have a very bright view of the future," Enkh Javkhlan says, and his face beams with hope at the prospect of a better tomorrow for his town and people.

For more information and gallery
wolfeconomy.asia